Just Walking Home:
Appalachian Trail Hikes 1996-2013

by

Robert C.A. Goff

Dreamsplice
Christiansburg, Virginia

Just Walking Home: Appalachian Trail Hikes 1996-2013

Copyright © 2019, 2023 by Dreamsplice

All rights reserved, including the right to reproduce this book, or portions thereof, in any form.

The map excerpts within this book are not intended to replace a full-size, printed map, and are used for illustration only. [North is toward the top of the map, unless otherwise indicated.] Trails are sometimes relocated, roads sometimes change, route numbers may change, roads previously designated with an occasional route number on a sign may now provide only a road name on its signs. Seeming landmarks (especially built structures) may change or vanish. For planning and travel, you should obtain the latest edition of an appropriate map.

Most hiking maps are based on a USGS topographical plot, showing the lay of the land and elevations. Although the USGS 7.5 minute quad maps show the finest detail (often down to individual farmhouses and sheds), they are most useful for a circumscribed hike within a relatively small area. USFS maps usually encompass a wider area, but often lack details that may be important to a hiker. For long stretches of only the AT, the specialized series of AT maps from the USFS and Appalachian Trail Convention (or "Conference") provide the greatest *linear* trail distance coverage for the pack weight. But they do not show much of the area surrounding the trail's right of way —just a "spaghetti" map of the AT, designed specifically for AT thru-hikers. For the widest areas of interest, such as a National Park or the Smokies region, a National Geographic—*Trail Illustrated* series map is an excellent investment, showing fine detail, named trails, surrounding communities, all regional roads and highways, as well as the background of the USGS topography. As with all printed maps, obtain the most current one available.

Image Credits:
    Richard M. Goff   *[RMG]*
    Robert C.A. Goff   *[RCAG]*

Map Credits (with page numbers):
    DeLorme (21)
    National Geographic – Trails Illustrated: (7, 57, 61, 71)
    Rand McNally: (23)
    US Forest Service: (9, 15, 49)
    US Forest Service and Appalachian Trail Convention: (75, 79)
    US Geological Survey: (43)

Dreamsplice
3462 Dairy Road
Christiansburg, VA 24073

www.dreamsplice.com/books

Cover design by Robert C.A. Goff, Copyright © 2019 by Dreamsplice
Front cover photo: 2012 of RMG at Angels Rest, above Pearisburg, VA. Photo by RCAG.

ISBN 13: 979-8-9867728-1-3
Library of Congress Control Number: 2019912381

First Edition: September 2019
Rev 2: November 2023

Contents

1996 Trail and Transformation: 5
   Bob solo: Giles County, VA AT night hike in a snow storm. (Philosophy and introspection. No photos.)

1997 Flat-Peter Trail: 9
   Bob solo: Giles County, VA, below Peters Mountain and around Kelly Flatts

Salt-Sulfur Turnpike: 15
   A wagon road to the past. Giles County into Monroe County, WV

1997 Springtime at War Spur Shelter: 22
   excerpts from the register, March and April

1998 AT Erwin TN to Damascus VA May: 23
   Bob, Richard and Mike

1998 Black bear darkens hiker's fun: 40
   A real-life bear tale (June)
           by Michael Hemphill

2000 AT Mt. Rogers VA April: 43
   Bob, Richard, Floyd and Shanghai loop hike

2001 AT Duncan Ridge GA April: 49
   Bob and Shanghai loop hike from AT

2003 AT Chestnut Knob VA Winter: 57
   Bob and Richard and Shanghai, on AT, near Burkes Garden VA

2004 AT Iron Mountain TN July: 61
   Bob, Richard, Micah, Floyd and Shanghai loop hike from Damascus VA along Iron Mountain Trail to AT

2010 AT Dragon's Tooth VA July: 71
   Bob and Micah, day climb up and back

2012 AT Angel's Rest VA September: 75
   Bob, Richard and Lynn, day climb up and back

2013 AT Peters Mountain VA June: 79
   Bob and Richard

Non-fiction by Robert C.A. Goff

> **Blend Your Own Pipe Tobacco: 52 recipes with 52 color labels**
> **How to Read a US Roadmap**
> **Climbing Out: Grand Canyon Hikes 1997-2006**
> **In the Ozone: collected essays, poems and non-fiction**

Fantasy-fiction by Robert C.A. Goff

> **Ternaria: Legacy of a Careless Age**

Science-Fiction by Robert C.A. Goff

> **Impact Mitigation and other Science-Fiction Short Stories**

Fantasy-fiction by Robert C.A. Goff and Micah M.A. Goff

> The Counterspell Chronicle
> > **Counterspell: Guardian of the Ruins**
> > **Counterspell: The Second Law**
> > **Counterspell: Age of Fool**s [upcoming]

Trail and Transformation:

A Winter Night-Hike on the Appalachian Trail

I have hiked portions of the Appalachian Trail in darkness. I seldom carry a flashlight. The tiniest sliver of moon offers plenty of light to hike by, once my eyes have fully accommodated to the dark. I enjoy the night sounds and the solitude—and the sense of having cast aside what is thought to be one of man's limitations. In my pack I carry a small candle lantern, strictly for emergencies. On this snowy, February afternoon, I had not intended to hike in darkness.

I parked off the road beside the AT, where it crosses VA 601, north of Newport, Virginia. The trail was blanketed in one-half foot of fresh snow.

From there, the descent into John's Creek Valley was a steady drop of 1300 feet over 2 miles—a forty-five minute walk, I estimated. I hefted my 38 pound backpack, took walking stick in hand, and began hiking at about 4:45. At nearly the same time, the snow shower of the previous night resumed its fury. I briefly looked back at the blue roof of my Bronco II, sinking beyond the horizon, wondering if this was a good idea. My pride in never being deterred by weather urged me on.

Amid the snow-spattered tree trunks and lofty horizons, the descent refreshed my enthusiasm. Eight inches of virgin powder cushioned each step as I moved steadily downhill. I noticed the white paint blazes that mark the route of the AT closely resemble patches of wind-blown snow clinging to the oak bark. I circled steeply into the brush uphill from the trail to bypass a large deadfall. The descent slowly continued into the blowing snow and rapidly fading daylight.

By the calendar, it was a new moon. Low, opaque clouds released their snow. As night closed in, I had nearly reached the bottom of the valley. Now, AT blazes had to be touched to distinguish them from random snow blotches. I continually thumped the trail with my stout, walnut walking stick. Even through eight inches of snow, I could clearly feel the difference between the resonant *thump* of striking the compacted surface of the treadway and the dissipated *thud* of the surrounding duff. My eyes could now distinguish only two qualities: dark tree and non-tree. I knew from having studied the topographical map the previous evening that there were no cliffs over which to blindly careen. There were, however, three creeks to cross in the darkness. The noise of the water, I reassured myself, would warn me as I approached a creek.

In John's Creek valley, the creeks flow through tunnels of giant rhododendrons. As the AT crosses the creeks, it is overarched by towering rhododendron branches. A distinctive feature of rhododendron is that it is evergreen. So while I took each laborious step through the February snow into the creek valley, the broad leafed surfaces of the rhododendron branches sagged further toward the ground, beneath the weight of their accumulating snow. In the first creek valley, they had drooped to the level of my chest, requiring me, with my 38 pound pack, to duck-walk beneath them. With each wrong move, a dozen leaves-full of snow dumped down the back of my neck. This first creek crossing was over a solidly built, wooden bridge, complete with railings and steps.

The second creek, again spanned by a well built wooden bridge, was easier than the first—and no drooping branches. My confidence grew. But by the time I had crossed it, the night had taken on the darkest dark I have ever experienced. With eyes wide open, I saw only the phantom phosphenes—ghost images generated by the random discharge of retinal nerve cells. Snow and tree, sky and earth, forward and backward—all appeared to be the same featureless deep black nothing. I felt no fear, only the sinking fatigue of realizing how long it would take to ascend 300 feet up the opposite slope, cross the remaining creek and reach War Spur shelter fifty yards beyond it.

The incessant *thump* of my walking stick kept me on the trail. The topo map had indicated no intersecting trails to lead me astray. And the slope determined the right direction on the *thump* trail. My strategy was that if even one step (or *thump*) did not feel convincingly like "trail", I would back up two steps and try again. Some areas were a breeze. Others required backing up repeatedly—as many as twenty or thirty times to advance ten feet. Once I felt along the bark of likely trees to determine if I could feel the texture of a latex paint surface—an AT blaze, but by then my finger tips were too cold to differentiate between smooth latex and merely cold, damp bark.

Just before the final creek, heralded by the raucous sloshing of rapids, the trail seemed to dead-end. I backed up and tried again for nearly twenty minutes, sometimes backtracking as much as fifty paces in the blackness in search of a missed turn. Finally I convinced myself that I was on the trail, even though it was impassable. Where the trail should have been, two and three inch thick horizontal rhododendron branches touched my shins and blocked the path above.

In anger and frustration, I swung my walking stick against the unseen obstructing branches. To the *swoosh* of a tiny avalanche, the offending branches raised up to the level of my chest. They had bent beneath the weight of so much snow that they had completely obscured the trail. The blow from my stick had released their burden.

I reached the final creek and surveyed the crossing with my blind-man's cane. Two slightly flattened logs seemed to be all that spanned the creek. Each felt about 8 inches in diameter situated about 10 inches apart. How far they stretched I could not determine. The span was longer than my walking stick. Six inches of snow covered the top of each log. I was reminded of the game of trying to guess the shape of an object rattling around inside a sealed cigar box. I smiled. I knew this object's shape—slippery!

After unfastening both my hip belt and my sternum strap as a safety precaution, I mounted the logs at the near end. With one foot on each log, toes widely out-turned like an exaggerated Chaplin impersonation, I rocked from side to side. Each step advanced one boot by about an inch. The logs sagged noticeably with each shift of my weight. My pack, now supported only by shoulder straps, slipped back and forth as I rocked. Rushing, icy water churned beneath me. My eyes saw nothing. In two minutes, I was across.

Twenty more minutes of stumbling and fumbling gained me the remaining fifty yards and the quiet safety of the open-face War Spur shelter. Its overhang was sufficient to prevent snow from reaching the raised floor. I unloaded my gear and brought out supper (all by "Braille"). Then I succeeded in doing what I had avoided throughout the hike. I spun around and smacked my head against the flat of the shelter's central support beam, fortunately made of smooth wood. Amazing how the aura of safety causes me to lower my guard.

After a supper of ready-to-eat food, I spread my sleeping bag on a pad and collapsed into the sleep of physical and mental exhaustion (interrupted several times by the hardy, "Arctic" mice that wait here through the long winter, like trolls beneath a bridge, in case someone might come along in a February blizzard).

The following morning I retraced my steps under a brightly overcast sky. The real excitement came in the first creek valley, with the log crossing. When I saw it all in sobering daylight, I audibly gasped. Had I seen this in the light of day prior to my hike, I would never—NEVER—have attempted it in a snow storm, in the dark, or just in the dark! Had I seen it in the light of my emergency candle lantern, I probably would have stopped there and pitched a tent in the snow, fifty yards from a dry shelter. Even though the logs only spanned about ten feet, a slip from them would surely have resulted in a broken bone on the partially submerged rocks below.

I am often asked why I would hike and backpack in "bad" weather. I hike year round, seldom checking a weather forecast before I set out. I prepare for what the weather might be. The weather and its hazards are part of the process of wilderness. I see backpacking less as a vacation than as an instrument of transformation, like a prophet wandering in the wilderness…like hiking alone in a snow storm in the dark, confident of how it will end, eager to experience the process of getting there, but not sure what the transformation will bring.

1996

A springtime view of where I parked on Route 601, in the snow, for my February night hike in 1996.

1997 Flat-Peter Trail

Bob solo: Giles County, VA, below Peters Mountain
(day hike)

[Published in abbreviated form in *New River Outdoors*, vol 1:2, Nov. 1997, p 8.]

Brief Description: A strenuous, 5-plus hour rectangular loop hike along the flank of Peters Mountain, including a portion of the Peters Mountain Wilderness. Easy 2 to 2.5 hour out-and-back of either the southern or eastern legs of the loop. Many established campsites. Beautiful creek crossings, fern fields, abundant wildlife. Many fossils (brachiopods common).

Location: Northeast Giles County, Virginia

Length: 9 miles

Elevation Change: 900 feet

Water: Many creeks along the trail (purify)

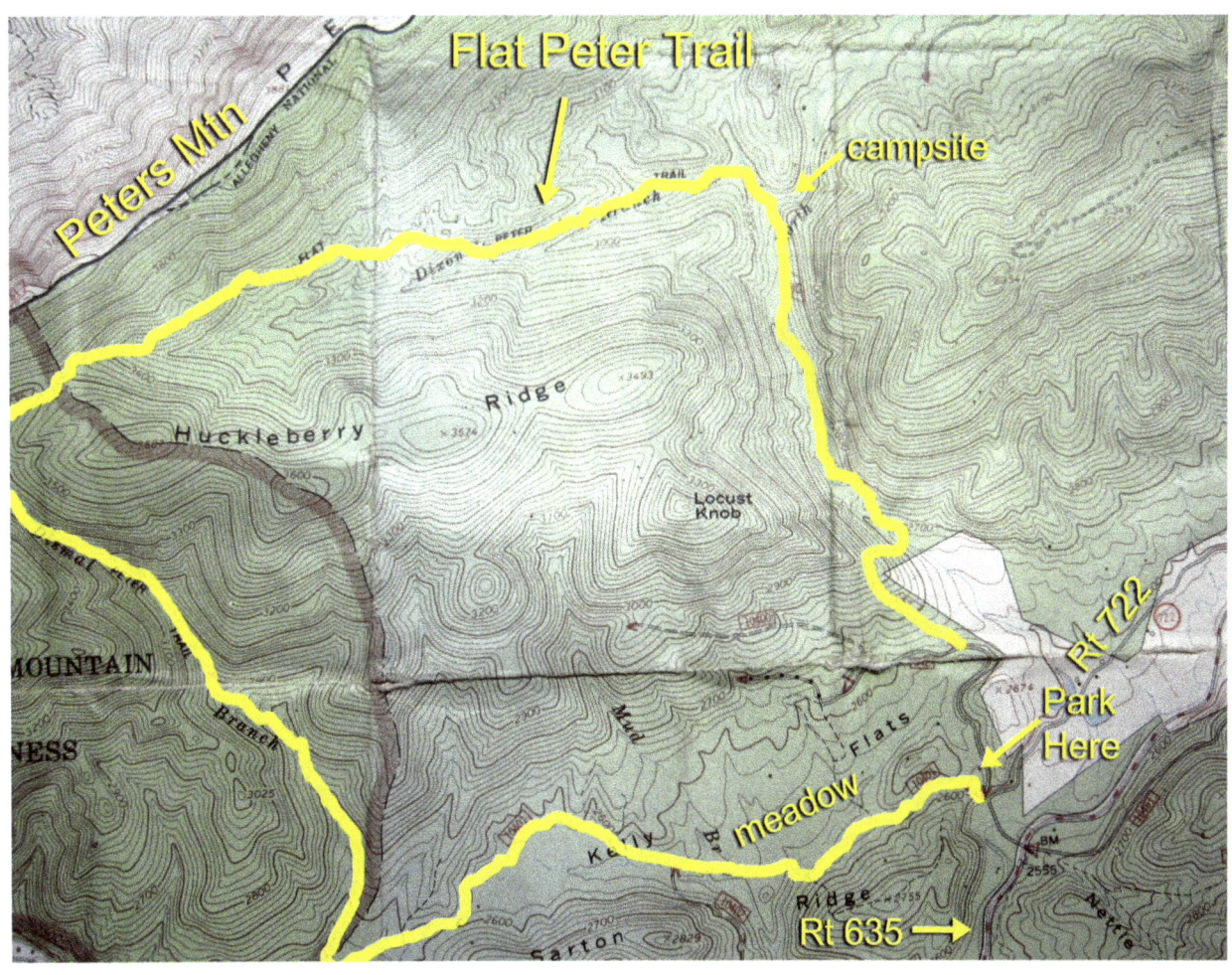

Map: USGS "Interior, VA" 7.5 minute quadrangle (Do not use the otherwise wonderful Jefferson National Forest Map for Blacksburg Ranger District. The trail location and intersections, as well as FS roads are incorrect for the area of this trail.)

Primeval Solitude

There are no panoramic vistas along Flat Peter Trail. Its scenes are of eastern highland forest at its most primitive. The trail receives very little traffic when compared to the nearby segment of Appalachian Trail passing through Peters Mountain Wilderness. Solitude, indeed, is one of its charms. The other is the incipient victory of wilderness over civilization. Gone, is almost all evidence of the railroad that once followed the eastern quarter of the trail. Train wheels, the only remnant, can be seen in the creekbed at the junction of Dixon Branch and North Fork. Another pair stands beside the trail just south of the campsite there. While all of the area (and all of Virginia) was logged in the distant past, three quarters of Flat Peter Trail passes through a succession of habitats as close to native as can be found anywhere in the region. Though not truly primeval, the aura of primeval is compelling, as one walks within rhododendron tunnels, repeatedly crossing creeks on mossy stepping stones. The trail wanders through stands of maturing hemlock, and ridges of oak-chestnut hardwood forest. The high saddle of the northern leg carries the hiker through a broad expanse of chest-high ferns. From the saddle, one could reach the Allegheny Trail by directly ascending north a quarter mile to the ridge of Peters Mountain. The western side of the rectangle, through the drainage of Dismal Branch, within Peters Mountain Wilderness, is so primitive as to be quite hazardous if descended (hiked counterclockwise) or during rainy weather. Storm damage, dating back to Hurricane Hugo, is most notable on the western leg, but is not a major obstacle to a hiker. (A full backpack increases the challenge, but the trail is still passable.) The gravel/dirt road comprising the southern segment of the trail winds through a series of scenic, narrow meadows in Kelly Flats.

Log bridge with a log handrail crosses the creek.

Nature has been so successful here in reclaiming its land that the trail had nearly ceased to exist two years ago. Then, a small group of hikers, calling themselves the "Backpackers and Bushwhackers," volunteered to begin the process of clearing and blazing the trail, and improving the treadway. I came across two of its members in September, carefully pruning back the undergrowth with hand loppers. Marsha Via (Blacksburg, VA) and Tom Spero (Radford, VA) have labored at this "very special" trail for the past two years, starting on the eastern leg. Their work, and that of a handful of fellow volunteers, has groomed the trail nearly to the saddle between Dixon Branch and Dismal Branch. This portion of the trail is, as a result, an almost effortless stroll. The only significant challenge to the hiker along this segment is the single-log bridge over North Fork. (With care, and a little apprehension, I successfully crossed it wearing a 55 pound pack.)

Proposed Relocation

It is unlikely that the western leg, which crosses through Peters Mountain Wilderness, will ever be cleared and marked any better than its present primitive state. According to Ranger William Compton, Program Director for the Blacksburg Ranger District, Jefferson National Forest, this portion of the trail is practically unmaintainable, given the proscription of the use of power tools in the Wilderness Area. The heavy storm damage there, and the location of sections of trail virtually within the bed of Dismal Branch, would be a major restoration project even with power equipment. The Blacksburg Forest Service Headquarters recently withdrew their trail pamphlet for Flat Peter Trail following a number of complaints by hikers who had either lost their way in the Dismal Creek section, or felt that the trail was unacceptably primitive. (I would describe it as wonderfully primitive!) On a recent evaluation of the trail, Ranger Compton himself was unable to locate the course of the trail in part of this area, and fell between two boulders up to his shoulders, without serious injury. (I experienced similar difficulties when *descending* the western segment.) His proposal, now under environmental impact assessment, is to keep the Dismal Branch segment open to the adventuresome, but leave it unmaintained. The primary route of the western leg would be relocated outside of the Wilderness Area, first tracing Huckleberry Ridge eastward, then descending the bank of the unnamed creek just east of the Wilderness Area boundary, eventually connecting with FS10401 a quarter mile east of its present intersection. He is proposing several other short, connecting trails that might eventually create another loop from the campsite on the northeast corner of the Flat Peter rectangle to Salt Sulfur Turnpike, a mile and a quarter farther east. These changes are one to two years away. [*Written in 1997.*]

Practical Matters

There are no toilet facilities anywhere along Flat Peter Trail or at its campsites. If you plan to hike the entire loop, or to stay overnight, bring along a small plastic trowel and toilet paper. Perennial water is available all along the trail from the many creeks, but like all water from unprotected sources, it should be treated. There are no trash receptacles, so plan to pack out (and carry home) any trash you create. Flat Peter makes a good weekend outing or a moderately strenuous day hike. Allow at least five hours for day hiking, or six hours with a full backpack. This is not a trail to attempt in darkness. Flat Peter is one of the rare trails on which I have repeatedly depended on a topographic map ("Interior, VA" 7.5 minute quadrangle). Carry a compass. You are never more than three miles from the highway, so if you can find South, you can find your way out without serious orienteering skills. If you plan to hike the entire loop, let someone know where

North Fork Creek.

you plan to go and when you plan to return. All that being said, Flat Peter Trail is a truly wonderful and unique treasure.

Getting There: Take US 460 "west" toward Pearisburg, VA to state route 635 (just east of the New River bridge near Ripplemead, VA). A sign indicates "White Rocks Recreation Area." Travel east on SR635 approximately 12 miles to Glen Alton Road (SR722). *Note that 5 miles from US 460, SR635 makes a left hand turn.* Follow SR722 for 0.15 miles. The right fork is a private road. Take the left fork, marked "Kelly Flats Road." Pull beyond the gated road to the left and park, being careful not to block the gates.

Kelly Flats.

Trail Directions: Flat Peter Trail forms a yellow-blazed rectangle, roughly 2.5 miles east to west and 2 miles north to south. FS10401, immediately to the left (west) when passing the "Kelly Flats Road" sign, forms the gently undulating, 2.5 mile southern leg of the rectangle. Follow this principal dirt/gravel road past the meadows and swamp of Kelly Flats. Where it ends, continue straight into the trees (not the right turn with the yellow trail marker). After a quarter mile, the trail intersects an abandoned roadbed. The left fork joins the Appalachian Trail in three quarters of a mile. The right fork, marked by a small "National Forest Wilderness" sign, is the western side of the Flat Peter Trail rectangle. This 2 mile leg ascends, sometimes steeply, the drainage of Dismal Branch. Some sections of the trail have been reclaimed by the creek, though much of the year, the water can only be heard beneath the rocks. The trail is not well marked along this leg, but this presents little difficulty, since it generally follows the fall line of the drainage. (See Proposed Relocation) *This western segment, as well as the northern segment, is significantly easier to follow when hiking the loop in a clockwise direction.* Watch for the yellow blazes. An established campsite is reached just before the trail turns northeast to begin the northern side of the rectangle. The westernmost portion of this poorly marked, 2.5 mile northern segment simply passes through the trough of the saddle between Peters Mountain and Huckleberry Ridge, after which the trail is well cleared and better marked. Again, this northern leg is easier to follow when completing the loop in a clockwise direction. At the point where Dixon Branch joins North Fork, there is a well-maintained campsite. From there, the 2 mile eastern side of the rectangle is generally an easy walk down a long-abandoned railroad grade, paralleling the creek on a clearly marked course. Just before reaching Kelly Flats Road, FS942, the trail steeply climbs then descends a small ridge. At the intersection with the road, continue left (southeast) for about 0.3 miles to reach the parking area.

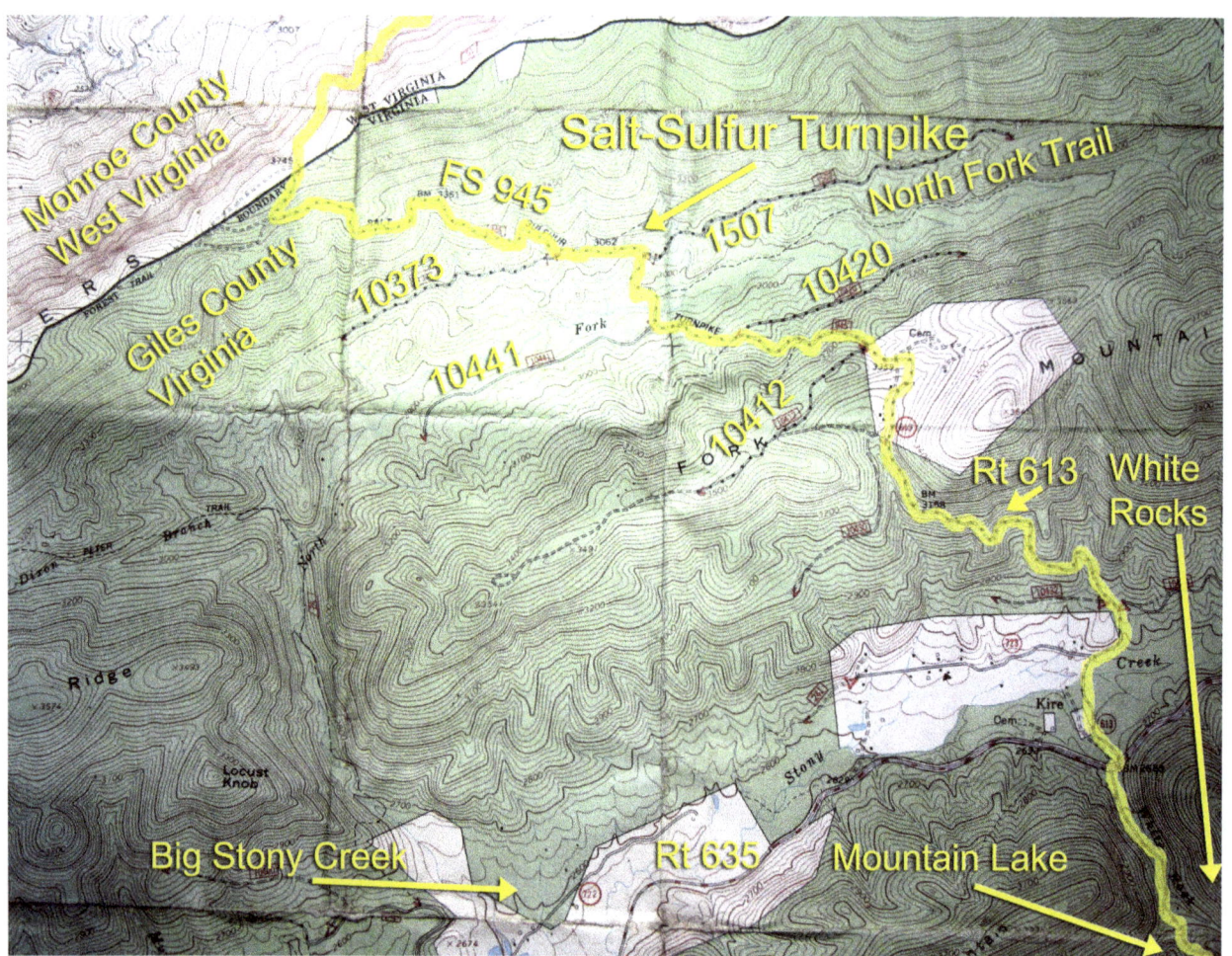

The Salt-Sulfur Turnpike today.

Salt-Sulfur Turnpike:

A wagon road to the past.
Giles County, VA into Monroe County, WV

History of the Salt-Sulfur Turnpike: Between 1859 and 1861, in an effort to connect the tourist spas of Yellow Sulfur Spring, near Christiansburg, VA, and Salt Sulfur Springs, near Union (West) Virginia, the counties of Giles and Montgomery, together with private interests, undertook the construction of a wagon road from the train depot in Cambria, Virginia, to Union (West) Virginia. It passed through Blacksburg to Newport, Virginia, then up Salt Pond Mountain, along the general route of state Route 700, to present day Mountain Lake. Passing *east* of the lake (not along the steep western shore where the present Route 613 is located), it ascended Potts Mountain, Fork Mountain and Peters Mountain.

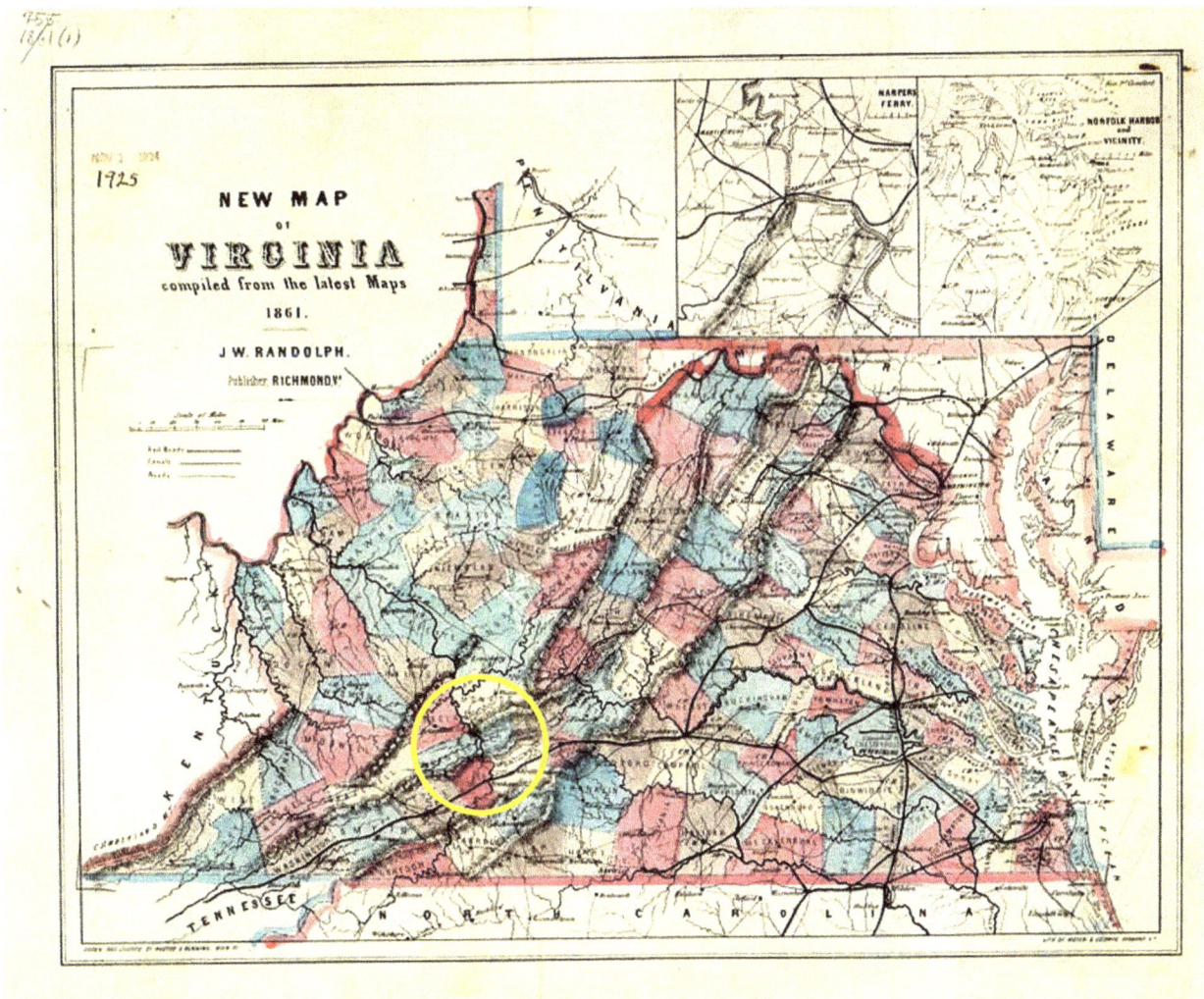

The Commonwealth of Virginia, before the Civil War. Education Library of Virginia.

[http://www.lva.virginia.gov]

The old wooden hotel at Mountain Lake functioned as a tourist way station between Cambria and Union. Spa tourists could reach Cambria by train from eastern Virginia, traverse the Salt Sulfur Turnpike, visit the spas at either terminus, then continue by train from Union. The new turnpike was to be a blessing to travelers, since no train tracks crossed the mountains during the mid-nineteenth century. Unfortunately, by the time the turnpike was completed, the two Virginia tourist centers which it was to connect were no longer in the same state. It simply became another difficult mountain road between two nations at war with one another.

The Salt-Sulfur Turnpike in the Civil War: During May of 1864, Union General George Crook (destined to capture the Chiricahua Apache chief, Geronimo, 22 years later) invaded Southwest Virginia with an army of over 6000. Of his three brigades, the First was commanded by (future president) Colonel Rutherford B. Hayes. Within Hayes' command was (future president) 1st Lieutenant William McKinley of the 23rd Ohio Volunteer Infantry. The Union plan was to bring an end to the war by destroying Virginia's primary supply of salt, mined at Saltville, and bullet lead, mined at Austinville (near Wytheville). Along with these, they would destroy the long bridge over the New River at Central Depot (now Radford), severing the only rail link to Eastern Virginia. This invasion was simultaneous with the Battle of the Wilderness, fought between Lee and Grant, further east.

After a fierce battle at Cloyds Mountain (just north of the municipal airport at Dublin), Crook did succeed in sacking Dublin, then military headquarters of Southwest Virginia, and burning the courthouse. Under Union pressure, Confederate soldiers set fire to the wooden long bridge, lest it fall under Union control. Crooks forces were unable, however, to take Saltville or Wytheville.

On learning of Grant's withdrawal from Lee's forces in northern Virginia, Crook ordered a hasty retreat to the North. He was turned away from the heavily fortified pass at Narrows, instead following Salt Sulfur Turnpike from Newport, up present day SR700 past Salt Pond (Mountain Lake) and continuing over Peters Mountain to Union (West) Virginia. His retreat was plagued by late snows and torrential rains. In the section of Salt Sulfur Turnpike between Salt Pond and the ridge of Potts Mountain (where the Appalachian Trail now crosses), his heavily laden wagons sank in mud above their axles. In the shadow of harassing Confederate gunfire, some of the wagons were intentionally destroyed. Others were saved only by dumping quantities of cannon shot and cases of Minie balls into the quagmire. This area (about 3 miles north of Mountain Lake) has since been known as Minie Ball Hill, and is marked by a large Forest Service marker on the roadside.

Why did this powerful invasion force retreat with so little provocation? We have two clues.
1. Crook graduated near the bottom of his class at West Point.
2. Theodore Roosevelt later stated, "McKinley has no more backbone than a chocolate eclair."

Brief Description: An historic wagon road excursion through some of Jefferson National Forest's more remote areas. The unpaved remnant of Salt Sulfur Turnpike extends from Mountain Lake, Virginia, in Giles county, across the mountain boundary, to West Virginia state highway 29 in Monroe county. Although the entire length is accessible to a narrow, high-clearance, four-wheel drive vehicle (whose owner doesn't care about scratches to the paint), it offers hikers access, via gated Forest Service roads and marked trails, to isolated mountain ridges and valleys, wilderness areas, a stand of virgin Hemlock, White Rocks Recreation Area and the Appalachian and Allegheny National Scenic Trails. All of the turnpike except the state boundary portion, high on Peters Mountain, may be driven without difficulty in a passenger car during most of the year. Many established campsites. Beautiful creek crossings, abundant wildlife. (I sighted an immature Broadwinged Hawk and immature Bald Eagle.) Covered bridge north of Newport, VA. Occasional Civil War artifacts (Minie balls). Many fossils (brachiopods, coral, gastropods, crinoids).

Location: Primarily Giles County, Virginia

Length: Original turnpike 45 to 50 miles. War Spur and Chestnut Trail 2.5 mile loop. Wind Rock 0.4 miles "north" on Appalachian Trail (AT). AT "south" to Bailey Gap shelter 3.5 miles. Loop hike AT "south" past Bailey Gap shelter to FS734 then back to turnpike and return to starting point at AT 10.2 miles. FS734 8 miles. FS10412 1.5 miles. FS10420 2 miles. FS10441 1 mile. North Fork trail 2 miles. FS1503 1.5 miles. FS10373 1 mile. FS945 (upper portion of turnpike) to state line 1.4 miles. Allegheny Trail SE from turnpike to AT on Peters Mountain 4.5 miles.

Elevation Change: +2000' between Newport, VA and Mountain Lake; -1200' between Potts Mountain and SR635; +1100' between SR635 and Peters Mountain; -1100' between Peters Mountain and WV Route 29. Side spurs usually show little elevation change. War Spur—Chestnut Trail Loop ± 700'.

Water: Many creeks. Treat all water.

Map: USGS "Interior, VA" and "Eggleston, VA" 7.5 minute quadrangles. USFS map of Jefferson National Forest, Blacksburg Ranger District (some state road designations have changed since this map was published).

Gravel section of the Salt-Sulfur Turnpike.

Cutting Edge of Transportation: The remnants of Salt Sulfur Turnpike, built in 1861, can be found in Giles county, Virginia, between Newport, Virginia, northward to Mountain Lake, and on into West Virginia. Built originally as a tourist road, it soon played a role in the Civil War. Today, the remaining segments extend northward from Mountain Lake, as SR 613, across the state boundary on Peters Mountain, and down the north slope to West Virginia state highway 29. While some visitors who reach Mountain Lake Resort will venture beyond the asphalt paving and onto the gravel portion of Salt Sulfur Turnpike (FS613 north), few go beyond the parking area to the War Spur-Chestnut Trail loop, two miles from the lake. With recent re-grading of the road, it is possible to drive a standard-clearance passenger vehicle from Mountain Lake across Potts Mountain and Fork Mountain to the flank of Peters Mountain, though high water conditions may stop a passenger car at Fork Branch, just before the final pitch. While the drive is a beautiful one in any season, the greatest value of Salt Sulfur Turnpike today is the access it provides to numerous hiking trails in Jefferson National Forest, and unpaved, grass covered, Forest Service roads. The gravel turnpike itself provides miles of scenic hiking and cross-country skiing.

Hikes off (and on) Salt Sulfur Turnpike:

War Spur—Chestnut Trail Loop: Parking area 2 miles north of Mountain Lake. Marked by large sign. Easy 2.5 mile loop through the Mountain Lake Wilderness Area to War Spur Overlook. Passes through a rare, virgin stand of hemlock, fir and spruce.

Wind Rock—AT—War Spur Loop: Fairly easy 7.7 mile loop. Park at either War Spur trail head (see above) or the AT parking area 5.8 miles north of Mountain Lake. From the AT, hike "north" (actually ENE) past Forest Service billboard 0.4 miles to spectacular Wind Rock Overlook. Continue on AT 1.25 miles just below ridge of Potts Mountain. AT turns south, passing Lone Pine Peak (an inconspicuous knoll) and intersects War Spur Connector in about 1 mile. Reach the War Spur parking area in another 1.25 miles. Follow scenic gravel turnpike north for 3.8 miles to starting point at AT intersection parking area.

AT—FS734 Loop: Easy 10.2 mile weekend backpacking loop. Parking area 5.8 miles north of Mountain Lake. Travel "south" (actually WSW) on AT for 3.5 miles to Bailey Gap shelter (has fire ring and privy). Blue blazed trail to spring heads west from shelter; alternate water trail originates from AT 0.1 mile farther "south" (actually NNW). On reaching FS734, head right (east) for 4 miles along the scenic gravel road to reach the turnpike (a poorly labeled 'T' intersection). Turn right (uphill) and climb 1.5 miles on steep flank of Potts Mountain to return to starting point beside AT intersection and parking area.

FS road 10412 is perfect for a night hike.

FS10412 Spur: Easy 1.5 mile stroll along the ridgeline of Fork Mountain. From SR635 travel north on Salt Sulfur Turnpike about 2 miles. A large Forest Service sign, just over the crest of Fork Mountain, marks the turnpike as "Salt Sulfur Road". FS10412 is the next road (gated) to the left (SW). There is no parking area nearby, but avoid blocking the gate. This grassy road has no obstructions, no unexpected turns, no gullies, and is perfect for night hiking in total darkness. Suitable tent sites can be found in a number of meadows along the way. The road ends in a long meadow at the 3541' peak of Fork Mountain's western ridge (no views).

FS10420 Spur: The first mile or so is an uninspiring walk down an undulating gravel road. Beyond that, it becomes clear that this road's major purpose is for timber sales. Not a fun hike.

FS10441 Spur: A pleasant 1 mile hike along the western valley of North Fork. Area of timber cutting at the end of the road.

North Fork Trail: Two miles of charming, meandering grassy road (eventually tapering into a narrow foot trail) above the eastern valley of North Fork. Trail head is the first pulloff right (east) after crossing North Fork (no bridge) on Salt Sulfur Turnpike. One hundred yards in, a "wildlife clearing," suitable for tent sites, opens to the north. Along the

FS road 10420 being prepared for timber sales.

course of the road are several additional "wildlife clearings." The Forest Service signposts for these clearings have been so riddled with bullets that they no longer support the weight of their tiny signs (which justify the making of a wildlife clearing). Water available from several mossy creek crossings (treat).

FS1507 Spur: Easy 1.5 mile, gradually ascending, gravel road along the lower flank of Peters Mountain. No meadows or suitable tent sites. Right pulloff about 0.25 miles after crossing North Fork.

FS10373 Spur: Beautiful 1 mile hike along a grassy road. This is the (gated) left turn just before the start of FS945, which is the final pitch of Salt Sulfur Turnpike. A spring is located on the uphill side of the road about 150 yards from the gate. Tent sites are available at the end of the road. A trail leads south from there, up a knoll, then continues downhill, almost due south, most of the way to the campsite on the Flat Peter Trail at the junction of North Fork and Dixon Branch.

FS945—Turnpike climbs to the state line: After the gated turn to FS10373, Salt Sulfur Turnpike becomes conspicuously narrower, steeper, and accessible only to high clearance, narrow, four-wheel drive vehicles. This portion of the turnpike is designated as FS945. It also makes a moderately strenuous, wonderful 1.4 mile (each way) hike to the ridge of Peters Mountain, where it simultaneously intersects the Allegheny Trail and the VA/WV state line. FS945 is an excellent study in mid 19th century road construction. In its lower segments, hikers can find large exposures of fossil coral, suggesting that Peters Mountain was a submerged coastal reef in the very distant past. Brachiopods and other fossils abound. If you drive this road, expect your paint to be scratched by the encroaching brush.

Salt Sulfur Turnpike in West Virginia: It is possible to drive from the ridge of Peters Mountain down its north face to West Virginia state road 29, but this is a narrow, steep, brutal course, that ends by passing through posted private property. I do not

Covered bridge along VA Rt. 700.

recommend the drive. The pack of domesticated dogs at the lower end should also dissuade even adventuresome hikers.

Covered Bridges: Drive north on US 460 past Newport, VA. Turn left onto SR700. On SR700, about 200 yards after turning off US 460, a covered kingpost bridge can be discovered to the left of the road. You can park nearby and walk to and through the bridge. Beyond that, if you turn right at the stop sign, then right onto SR604, you will see another fairly well preserved wooden kingpost bridge. Wooden bridges were covered in order to protect the wooden support structure from decay.

Practical Matters: Perennial water is available all along the trail from the many creeks, but like all water from unprotected sources, it should be treated. During moderate snows, the turnpike may be traveled by four-wheel drive vehicles from Mountain Lake to as far as the crest of Potts Mountain. (From there northward is used by hearty souls for a sled run.)

Timberframe construction of the Rt. 700 bridge.

King-post support in the Rt. 700 bridge.

Following heavy rain, Fork Branch can not be crossed with a passenger vehicle.

Getting To the Salt-Sulfur Turnpike: From Blacksburg, VA, take US 460 west to SR700 (just past Newport). Follow signs to Mountain Lake. While most of SR700 follows the course of Salt Sulfur Turnpike, the unpaved portion begins at the north end of Mountain Lake. The turnpike may also be reached by going toward Pearisburg, VA to state route 635 (just east of the New River bridge near Ripplemead, VA). A sign indicates "White Rocks Recreation Area." Travel east on SR635 approximately 14 miles to SR613 (N to Peters Mountain, S toward Mountain Lake). *Note that 5 miles from US 460, SR635 makes a left hand turn.* The West Virginia end of the turnpike is posted as private property (though the claim is unclear).

Covered bridge on VA Rt. 604.

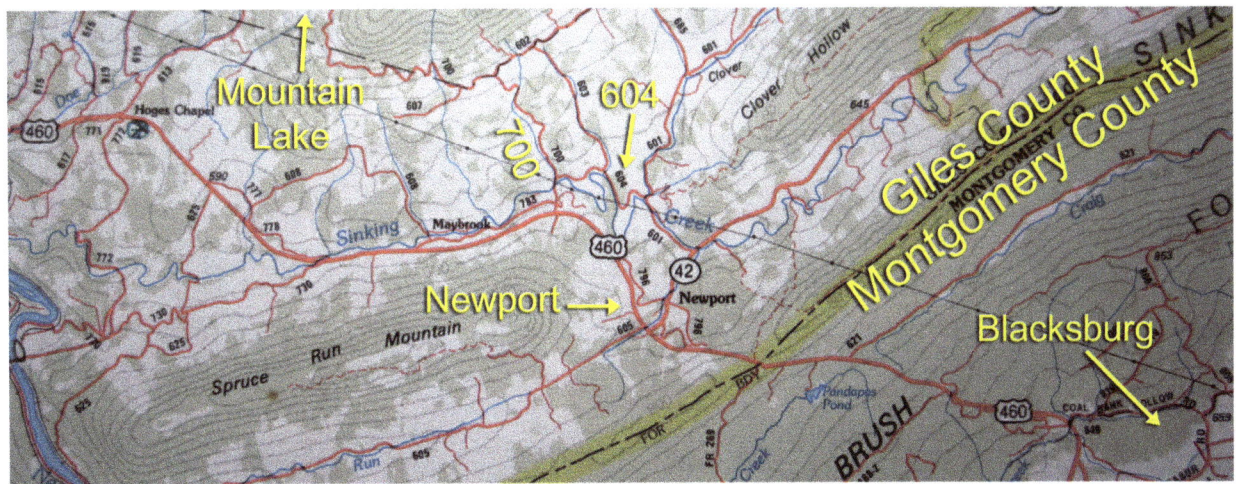

*To find the **covered bridges**, take 460 west (north) out of Blacksburg, then turn east at Route 700, toward Mountain Lake. They are both in that immediate valley.*

Springtime at War Spur Shelter:
excerpts from the shelter register, March and April 1997

3/2/97   "This place is so cool we decided to stay again after we hiked to Wind Rock. Actually, we are just lazy bums, but that's cool in itself."
Pink Dog & Turtle

3/9/97   "Not a bad day to be out and be in good health."
Clyde Perdue

3/13/97   "...looks like the mice got to the TP before I did....Gotta luv rhododendron leaves!"
Bevis

3/15/97   "Great shelter....great to be outside."
Mike & Matt

3/22/97   "Hiked in from Mountain Lake....Weather is amazing--breezy & sunny--great shelter. What a day to be in the mountains."
Jennifer & Kenney, Whitny & Molly

3/28/97   "Great shelter. In search of the elusive wild turkey. Heard four proud gobblers waking the woods at 5:55 am. Nothing more beautiful than a Spring gobbler in strut...."
Anon.

3/29/97   "...weekend trek. Beautiful weather, trail, spirits. I hope I don't see anyone."
Jim & Toast

3/29/97   "Beautiful day to be out. Came up to check our section of trail and the shelter. Special hike today; first hike with our 7 month old; he really seems to enjoy hiking."
Bill, Kellie, Cody and Colin and Stacey & Amber

4/4/97   "Troop 8 from Monroe NC is grateful for the AT volunteers...."
Anon.

4/17/97   "Cool uranium on the decaying tree stumps. Adds flavor to being at WARspur."
Curious George

4/17/97   "Snow flurries....melts the second it hits the ground."
Gator and Jake

4/18/97   "Suddenly it's clear in the 60's again."
Wahoo

4/22/97   "Virginia is kind of wet."
Broken Road

4/22/97   "It's raining again. And I sent my rain poncho home."
Lynx

4/23/97   "...still in my crispy, toasty sleeping bag. A lazy man is a happy man."
Pilgrim

May 1998: AT Erwin TN to Damascus VA

Bob, Richard and Mike
(9 days; ~100 miles)

Our party consisted of three hikers, all past the half-century mark. I (Bob Goff, alias Stogie) had planned the itinerary. My brother, Richard Goff, and his colleague, Mike Gregg, both professors of Engineering Fundamentals at Virginia Tech (Blacksburg, VA), had reluctantly agreed to the ambitious plan. We would drive to Erwin TN and begin the hike about mid-day at Indian Grave Gap, expecting to make Cherry Gap Shelter that evening. Each of the following three days would require that we cover about 14 miles. The remainder of the 10 day hike would be at a more leisurely pace.

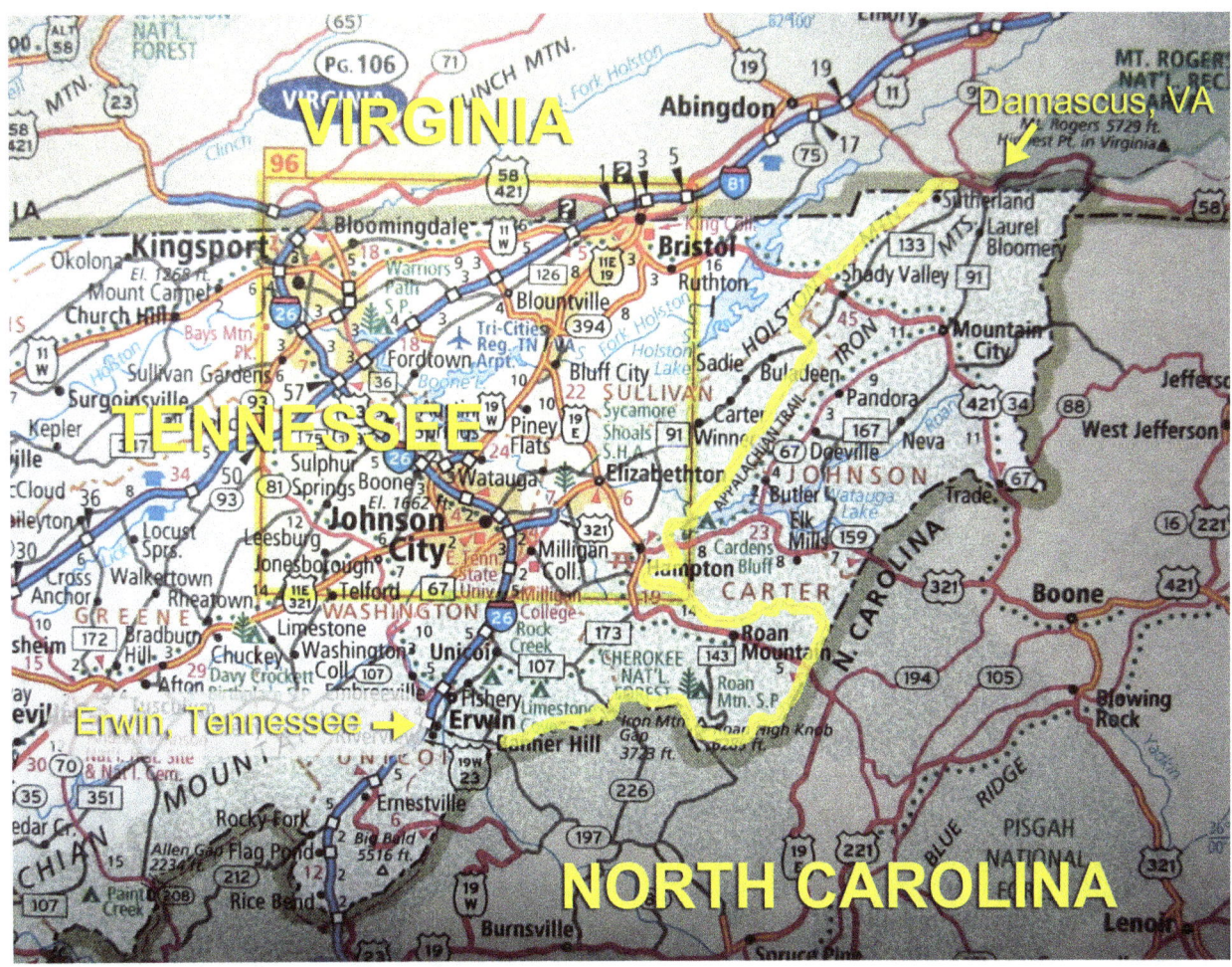

What I had not taken into account was the brutal ascent and descent of Roan Mountain. To make things a little more dicey, our planned stop in Hampton TN on the morning of day six had been coordinated with a rendezvous between Mike and his wife, Wendy. Once the difficulty of the hiking for days two and three became apparent, there was no easy way to modify the meeting time or date.

In the AT hiker tradition, this narrative will refer to members of our party by their "trail" names. I'm Stogie (something to do with the countless cigars I smoke, and my hand carved, solid walnut Marsh Wheeling Deluxe Stogie walking stick). Richard is Raudy (goes way back). Mike acquired his trail name along the way.

Stogie Staff.

Raudy, Stogie and Mike.

Day 1: Friday (5/22/98)

Hiked from Indian Grave Gap north. First hill was a killer. Weather was wonderfully warm, but overcast. Threatened to rain at Beauty Spot, where views were fairly limited by the low clouds. Raudy (Richard) and soon-to-be Chocolate Noodle (Mike) both seem in better shape than me, despite weeks of preparation.

Mike and Raudy at a cloud-obscured Beauty Spot.

Arrived late, though still light, at Cherry Gap Shelter. All tent sites taken by a youth-Wilderness Adventure group—Sulaho from New Dominion School in Dillwynn VA, a

Mike crosses a fence style. [RMG]

Unaka Mountain. [RMG]

group of 15 that we would see repeatedly over the next few days. Several of the Sulaho boys, who had taken up spots within the shelter, immediately cleared the shelter without prompting. Some even assisted my hiking mates by carrying their gear into the shelter. The boys were never boisterous or even typical-teenage-crude. In fact, they were asleep before the through-hikers in the shelter had settled down.

When Mike finally got his stove to boil water, he immediately dumped in a packet of chocolate Instant Breakfast (by mistake in the darkness). His noodle dinner became chocolate noodle dinner, and his trail name instantly became *Chocolate Noodle*.

This was Raudy's first chance to try out his new Camptrails nylon water bag. It fills easily at the spring, allowing him to sit in comfort at the shelter while he pumped the water through the Sweetwater filter. The bag seemed well worth the money if you pump your water. Since I use PolarPure iodine to treat water in my MSR Dromedary bag, there was no advantage for

Mike, eating his chocolate noodles. [RMG]

me to having yet another bag.

By the time we tried to get to sleep, the shelter, which holds six, was filled. This was the first of several nights during which I would toss and turn at the noisy proximity of other hikers in a shelter. My preference for years has been to sleep alone in my tent. I find my tent more comfortable, more bug-free, warmer in winter and cooler in summer, quieter, and a lot more private (if, say, I want to sleep in briefs on top of my sleeping bag).

Cherry Gap shelter.

Day 2: Saturday (5/23/98)

The top of my head was sore this morning. Cherry Gap Shelter has massive rafters about 4 feet above the floor. Saves cinder blocks, but my bald head really takes a beating. Because of the 14 miles of climbing ahead, I wanted to start without breakfast. I was vetoed. After our late start, we hiked in rain. The rain wasn't terribly cold, but it drenched the spirit. It did manage to bring out some gaudy orange-red salamanders. Chocolate Noodle zoomed ahead of us. We finally found him waiting at the side trail to Clyde

Salamander enjoying the rain.

Trail near Clyde Smith Shelter.

Rain gear comes out of the packs.

Smith Shelter. We hiked the "0.1 mile" to the shelter for a break. It was so tempting to just stay there for the night, but then we would be irreparably behind on our itinerary. We would push on to Roan High Knob Shelter. *Osprey*, another vintage, section hiker, said we were crazy. The boys from New Dominion School

Sulaho members at Clyde Smith shelter.

Climbing Little Rock Knob.

arrived. They too would spend the night at Clyde Smith.

After lunch and a little rest, Raudy, Chocolate Noodle

View from Little Rock Knob. [RMG]

Chocolate Noodle at Hughes Gap. [RMG]

and I trudged on toward Roan High Knob. The first shock was a little nubbin on the topo map called Little Rock Knob. Ha! It was soooo steep. It required hand over hand climbing in several spots, then an equally steep descent. I was ahead of the others until Hughes Gap. From there, Raudy and Noodle disappeared in front of me, not to be seen again until day's end. Steep, steep switchbacks. Relentless climbing. When I stumbled into Ash Gap, hardly able to keep my pack from tipping me over backwards, I was thrilled to see that Raudy and Noodle had decided to stop there for the night, still 1000 vertical feet and 1.3 miles from the summit of Roan Mountain. It seemed a pity to quit so close to our goal, but my tank was empty. Raudy went for water. He swears it was a brutally long water trail, but I don't know if the day's exertion might have

Campsite at Ash Gap.

tainted his assessment. There were no stars, but no rain either. My tent was up in two minutes. I prepared my dinner, shoveled it down, then (after hanging my food) collapsed into a dead man's sleep. We had pitched our tents at the Ash Gap campsite, near a number of couples out for the Memorial Day weekend.

Day 3: Sunday (5/24/98)

I slept like a stone. We started late. Chocolate Noodle left ahead of us. On climbing those final 1000 feet to the summit, I thanked my lucky stars that I had not attempted it in the twilight (and eventual darkness) the previous night. Although we never had to haul our packs up by rope, it was a close call in several spots.

It took me and Raudy two hours to hike that 1.3 miles. At the top, we detoured to the Skyland Hotel site, finding potable running water in the restroom

Raudy climbs Roan Mountain on the AT.

Restrooms at Skyland Hotel site parking lot.

alongside the parking lot. A little boy there asked if we were hiking "barr trails," which is apparently any trail his father didn't want him to wander down. No views in the fog. Further on, at the dreary Roan High Knob Shelter, we saw no note from Noodle. That shelter would have been tough to find in the dark.

Inside, books and papers were scattered about.

We descended the long, steep, rocky trail to Carvers Gap, where we found Chocolate Noodle near a large,

Carvers Gap (NC-TN border), 5512 feet elevation.

nearly full parking lot. The paved highway there seemed to maintain a steady stream of traffic. Noodle prevailed upon a couple about to depart for home to phone his wife and let her know we might be a few hours late reaching Hampton on the 27th.

Rocky descent beneath Roan High Knob Shelter.

Stogie atop the log steps above Carvers Gap. [RMG]

Round Bald was a steep climb up log steps. It was another climb to Jane Bald, then steep-steep downhill until Roan Highland Shelter, now called Stan Something Shelter. It was dreary, stinky, fly-filled, and right on the trail. Raudy and I caught our breath, then pushed on to "the Barn" (Overmountain Shelter).

Raudy at Stan Murray Shelter (old Roan Mtn. Shelter).

Overmountain Shelter ("the Barn").

Chocolate Noodle, we were told, had continued on for Doll Flats. We were tired, and the view too beautiful from the Barn. The Sulaho Wilderness Kids arrived, bringing Raudy's lost Capilene shirt. Great kids!

This afternoon, I discovered that all the blackberries at high altitude have no thorns. I'm told that if you transplant them to a lower altitude, they grow thorns.

Day 4: Monday (5/25/98 Memorial Day)

We left the spectacular views of Overmountain Shelter (The Barn). We had awakened with first light, cooked

Stogie, looking down at the Barn. [RMG]

Big Hump.

Noon break at Applehouse Shelter.

a quick breakfast, then departed. The climb north from the shelter is a long hike over steeply inclined meadows, about a mile and a half of it visible from the Barn. By mid-morning, we had climbed Little Hump and Big Hump. Off the back shoulder of Big Hump, we met a hiker who said that Chocolate Noodle had slept there, then departed about an hour prior to our

Raudy double-poles above Applehouse.

Raudy on a bridge "North" of 19E.

arrival. Raudy and I drove ourselves to catch up. By Apple House Shelter, we were both blown out, so we lolled about for 2 hours without boots, lying in the sun. I bathed in the creek. The Wilderness Kids (Sulaho) arrived to stay for the night. I took a group photo of the kids, and promised to post it on the internet. They were excited about that. Raudy and I left Apple House at about 3 pm, driving for the campsite at Sugar Cove.

Raudy crosses a fence on a ramp style.

The map and its elevation chart don't even agree on the landmarks, not to mention the mileage. We arrived at Sugar Cove at about 7:30pm. After 13.5 miles, we

were fairly beat up. Still no Chocolate Noodle. We weren't sure if he was still on the trail.

Campsite at Sugar Cove.

Stogie crosses a fence on a ladder style. [RMG]

Day 5: Tuesday (5/26/98)

We departed Sugar Cove campsite at about 10:30am. Boy! the trail today was difficult, despite the benign

Five-foot blacksnake.

Raudy vanishes into a Rhododendron tunnel.

Thru-hikers arrive at Moreland Gap Shelter after dark.

appearance on the topo and profile maps. Actually, today I removed my watch and never looked at the map. We passed a solo south-bounder named Scott, who had bummed food and rope from friends, and decided to do a week-long hike while awaiting his final "student check" for the summer. He was overloaded with Pop-Tarts, and gave each of us a package.

Today seemed harder than yesterday. It was actually heartening to see five thru-hikers arrive at the shelter as tired as I felt. Chocolate Noodle left a note. He plans to be in Hampton tomorrow AM. We'll get there about mid-day. We may spend the night at the hostel. At least we'll get a shower and good food. Five more days to Damascus.

Day 6: Wednesday (5/27/98)

It was a crowded, noisy night at the shelter. We got up to leave at dawn, then thunderstorms kept us there 'til 7:30. At that point, we just ducked our heads and stomped out into the storm. It stopped raining by the time we reached the fire tower. The gentle descents on the map all seemed to be steep uphills. Squishing our boots downhill, we reached Dennis Cove.

A note on the trail warned not to go to "Laurel Creek Hostel," claiming it's a scam. Later we learned that they charge resort prices for everything. The trail into Laurel Creek Gorge warned that one of the bridges was washed out. So we backtracked to the highway and headed west. Met "Bob" at Kincora Hostel. He had picked up Chocolate Noodle the previous day! Seems he was exhausted and seriously dehydrated (not surprising, consider the pace he had set for himself). Bob drove us (along with a Teva-wearing thru-hiker named "Inbetween") into Hampton, where we each got a private room with bed and sheets at $15 each at the Braemar Castle Hostel, owned by Sutton Brown, who also runs the hardware store and adjacent grocery. In town, we learned that Noodle had apparently left the trail and returned home. Raudy called to speak with him, and all was well.

Raudy pumps water above Laurel Fork Gorge.

Kincora Hostel.

The shower was also the laundry. I wore my clothes into the shower, scrubbed them with soap, took them off, and rinsed them, then washed myself. Raudy and I walked to a nearby diner and gorged ourselves on heaping plates of greasy foods.

It was at "the Castle" that Raudy and I both, simultaneously experienced the lightweight backpacking epiphany. Each of us jettisoned at least 12 pounds of crap from our packs. We looked at what

Braemar Castle Hostel in Hampton, TN.

Raudy at Braemar Castle Hostel.

we had not touched in five days, at food quantities, at extra doodads, just-in-case stuff, and even at books. Even though we had planned to resupply at Hampton, each of had walked into town with enough food to go another several days. We ceremoniously stuffed it all into a large cotton stuff sack (that Raudy had been carrying) and hung it in a closet at "the Castle," to be reclaimed after the hike.

Day 7: Thursday (5/28/98)

Sutton drove us to the trail at US 321. We missed Laurel Fork Gorge and Pond Flats. Raudy and I moved along the bottom of Lake Watauga and crossed the dam. At Lake Watauga Shelter, we noted an abandoned sleeping bag in the rafters. Seemed like a good quality Marmot. Raudy slipped from the steps and rolled to

Stogie at Watauga Lake. [RMG]

Raudy at Watauga Lake Shelter. A nice, abandoned sleeping bag hangs from the rafters.

Rolled earth dam at Watauga Lake.

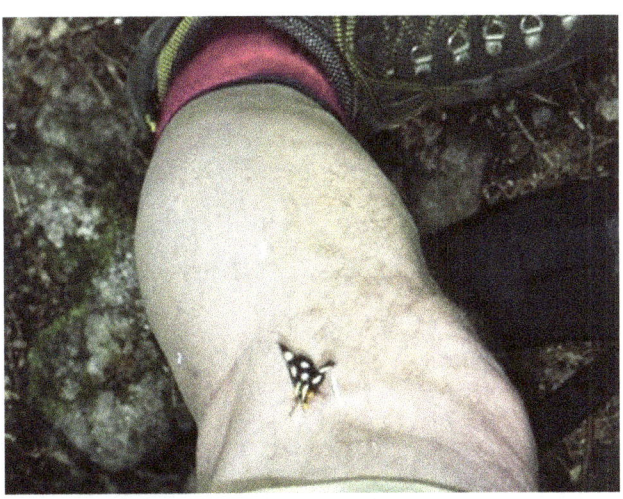
A moth licks sweat from my leg.

the ground. No serious hurts. Long, slow ascent to the ridge of Iron Mountain. Took water from a spring along the trail about 2 miles south of Vandeventer

View from Watauga Dam.

Shelter. A couple (man was Wild Hair, woman was Raincheck) and Inbetween were there. We pitched tents on the overlook behind the shelter. Water trail here is about 1 mile (all overgrown) round trip. We had beautiful, dry weather all day. Apparently 33 miles left to Damascus. With our new, lighter pack weights, both of us hiked faster and felt less fatigue at the end of the day.

Raudy pumps water before climbing to the ridge of Iron Mountain.

Tiny tent site behind Vandeventer Shelter. [RMG]

There is very little room at Vandeventer for putting up a tent, other than beside the fire circle. We managed

View of Watauga Lake from behind Vandeventer Shelter.

to squeeze our two tents between the back of the shelter and the rocky dropoff. Mosquitoes were a big problem for the three folks sleeping inside the shelter.

Day 8: Friday (5/29/98)

In accordance with Wingfoot Bruce's scheduled whippoorwill appearance, we were awakened at 5:30 am by a lone whippoorwill on the fire ring. Wild Hair threw something at it. Raudy and I left at about 7:45 from Vandeventer, determined to reach Double Springs Shelter (15 miles). That would put us within shooting distance of Damascus tomorrow.

We started north on the flat, grassy segment of the AT known as the Tennessee Turnpike, because of the ease

Yes. A bear does shit in the woods. [RMG]

The "Tennessee Turnpike".

of traveling at high speed. Raudy was unceremoniously attacked by a male grouse which circled his face, causing him to spin around and fall over. There is a long waterless stretch between Vandeventer and just before Iron Mountain Shelter. We did find a gurgling spring beneath the surface of a swamp. Couldn't fit a cup into the opening in the duff, so we fed in Raudy's pump tube and pumped out the water. Lunch at Iron Mountain shelter. Wild Hair and Raincheck leap-frogged us all day.

Apparently last night, two night hikers who noisily passed the Vandeventer later were challenged by a mother black bear. Wolfman drove it away by whistling a tune. He said it energized them to hike on. We saw bear droppings in the same area.

Monument to Uncle Nick Grindstaff. "Lived alone. Suffered alone. Died alone."

Inbetween decided to take her time getting to Damascus, since she couldn't make it by 11am tomorrow, when the Post Office closes. Raudy unloaded some extra food on her.

We arrived at Double Springs at 6:10pm, and set up at the grassy campsite about 80 yards "north" of the shelter. We planned to go for Damascus tomorrow (18 miles).

Day 9: Saturday (5/30/98)

We packed and were on the trail by 8:15am. Today was my turn to have a grouse scare the wits out of me. This one was a female, doing the "broken wing" ploy. Sort of downhill all day. Very fast. When we reached the US highway (421) by surprise, we calculated a rate of about 2 mph, nearly double our rate of the first half of the hike. Met some bikers at the summit there. An unmarked, piped spring is behind the trashy, cement picnic table there.

Campsite at Double Spring Shelter.

Raudy and I made it to Abingdon Gap shelter by noon, where we rested for about 40 minutes. The trail from

Picnic table with a spring behind it—US 421.

Stogie and Raudy at Abingdon Gap Shelter.

here to Damascus is one long downhill. About five miles before Damascus, I spotted an Eastern Diamondback Rattler lying across the trail. It was definitely alive, but seemed moribund. The temperature was warm enough for it to be moving faster. Instead, it lay still, with a slight recurve behind the head. The remainder of the body was not coiled. It never rattled, but held its rattle (~9 segments) slightly off the dirt. We circled it widely, and continued on.

Rattlesnake on the trail, holding rattle high.

About two miles from Damascus, I pulled a groin muscle, and strained the ligaments in my left knee. This was, I am certain, from moving too fast on the long downhill. Just before reaching Damascus, we descended through about 300 yards of extensive

storm damage, mostly cleared from the treadway. Once in Damascus, we walked immediately to the outfitter (Mt. Rogers Outfitters), outside of which stood two soda machines. We drank up. Then hiked to "The Place," where the car had been parked. We unloaded all our gear into the car, then went for dinner at the Pizza restaurant. Both of us had pecan pie a la mode first, then lasagna.

The drive home was preceded by a drive back to Hampton to recover our 25 pounds of abandoned crap, left hanging in the closet of the Braemar Castle. We decided that 100 miles in 9 days was not too bad for our ages and state of physical conditioning prior to the hike.

A real-life bear tale

Black bear darkens hiker's fun

by Michael Hemphill

*[first published in the New River Valley Current 6/2/98,
reprinted with permission of The Roanoke Times]*

An Appalachian Trail hiker met a hungry bear in Giles County. Guess who went hungry that night.

PEARISBURG--Hopefully, Rich Haveland's hike along the Appalachian Trail is ending better than it began.

Last Thursday, the second day of his southward-section hike from Craig County's Sinking Creek to Mount Rogers, Haveland almost became the entree to a hungry bear's dinner.

Haveland would later tell fellow hikers that around 7 p.m., as he was settling into his tent at Big Horse Gap near Sugar Run Mountain, he heard a rustling outside. He peeped through his tent, and there, looming larger than life to the 30-ish Connecticut man, stood a black bear nosing for an easy meal.

Fear made Haveland make a hiker mistake. He started throwing food at the bear, not realizing he was simply whetting the hungry creature's appetite. As one wildlife expert explained, "A bear doesn't understand that, 'There's more food there, and I can't have it.'"

Afraid the bear wanted a man-size helping, Haveland fled down the trail. Three hours later, he arrived at Wood's Hole, a hiker hostel about a half-mile off the trail run by Tillie Wood.

"He said the next morning, 'I was screaming, yelling and cussing that bear, and he kept coming,'" Wood recalled. "When he got here he was white as a ghost, his pulse was racing, he was scared to death."

(The bear may not have been his only cause for fright. After fleeing his site, he wandered lost for hours along a Forest Service road. Finally, he spotted a car and flagged it down. But lacking his backpack and camping gear, he didn't look like the typical hiker. Suspicious, one of the car's occupants pulled a gun on him while another frisked him for weapons before agreeing to drive him to Wood's Hole.)

That night Tillie Wood had 13 hikers staying with her. Haveland was the 14th. She usually offers breakfast only to the first eight, but Friday morning she made an exception.

He later returned to his camp site with Frank Gough, a Virginia game warden, to find his tent shredded and his gear destroyed. Gough helped him get resupplied at a local store--food, cooking gear, clothes, but no new tent.

"He said he'd just get a trash bag and make do as is," Gough said.

About the bear attack, Gough said, "I've been here several years and this is the first call of this sort I've had."

Gough has turned over the situation to Larry Crane, a wildlife biologist with the Virginia Department of Game and Fish. Crane said another hiker spotted the same bear Saturday night. He's cautioning trail travelers to be sure to stash their food up trees, out of a bear paw's reach. He said he won't try trapping the bear because he might snag an innocent animal.

This is the time of year when young bears, about 1½ years old and weighing between 75 and 125 pounds, are forced from their families to fend for themselves, Crane said. And they'll take an easy meal when they can get it.

If the bear sightings continue, Crane plans to head to Big Horse Gap, stoke up a fire and fry some bacon. Should the savory scent attract a furry visitor, he will shoot it with a tranquilizer dart to "educate it."

"After that encounter, most likely he'll decide he doesn't want to come around humans" and will learn to forage in the wild for food, Crane said.

As for Haveland, who earned the dubious nickname of "Bear-bait" from fellow hikers, he is back on the trail, heading south to where his car awaits him near Mount Rogers.

Hope the hike is un-bearable.

Wood's Hole Hostel, Pearisburg, VA.

Hiatus.

2000: April AT Mt. Rogers VA

Bob, Richard, Floyd and Shanghai loop hike
(3 days, ~31 miles)

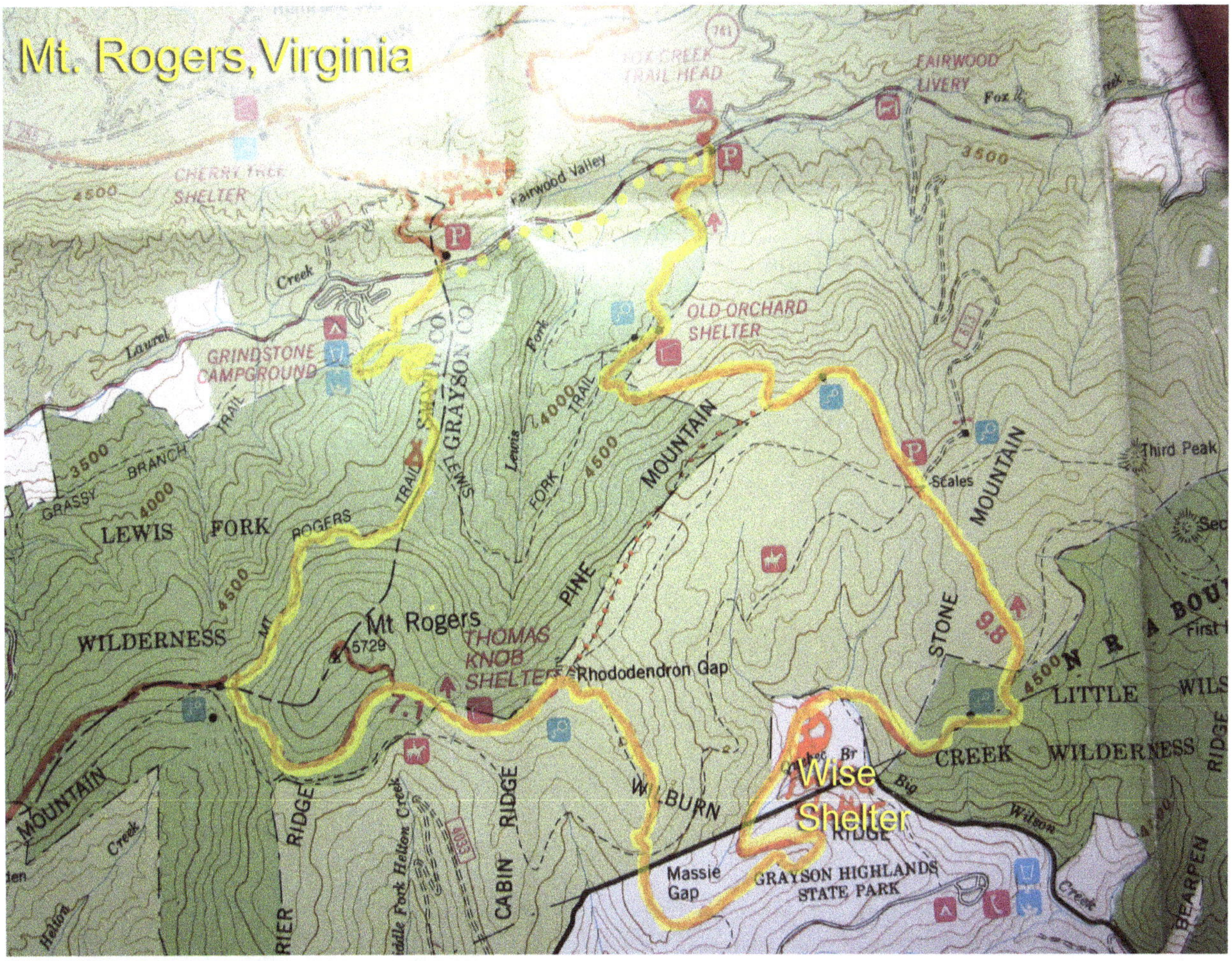

We parked near the Grindstone Campground, at a small parking area where the AT crosses VA state highway 603. Heading "south" on the AT, we hiked past Old Orchard Shelter, to reach a large campsite about 5.5 miles south of the highway.

Shanghai rests on the northern slope of Mt. Rogers after the first day of hiking. She is a Sharpei mix, rescued as a puppy from a Humane Society Shelter. She absolutely loves trail hiking. She may change her mind once I get a Woofer pack. [Spoiler: She didn't.]

Raudy and his Sierra Designs Clip Flashlite tent of many a trek. This is a campsite about 2 miles "south" of Old Orchard shelter. Room enough for a Scout troop. It's about 5.5 miles "south" of the AT access parking area off state highway 603.

Raudy offers a treat to Shanghai (my boss), and Floyd (Raudy's boss). Notice the huge fire ring at this campsite.

In the highland balds, the AT blazes are marked on wooden posts anchored in a small stone pile. [RMG]

After Shanghai and Floyd barked at some passing hikers, Raudy felt it timely to relate the history of the "Tomb of the Barking Dog". They listened attentively.

No primitive creek crossings here. Raudy photographs wildlife.

Shanghai emerges from the darkness of a rhododendron tunnel.

Shanghai and Floyd prefer the scenic route.

Mt. Raudy in the foreground. Mt. Rogers on the horizon.

With Raudy in the lead, the dogs tended to sprint back and forth between us.

Feral horses roam the highlands of Mt. Rogers and Grayson Highlands. Despite their "wild" state, they are accustomed to hikers and their handouts. If Shanghai's tail were longer than its stubby 4", it would have been between here legs, as we approached the horses. (far right) She would wait for me, before proceeding and closer. Raudy is among the horses, with Floyd nearby.

Raudy walks in the morning mists at Thomas Knob shelter.

It was at the Thomas Knob shelter that we encountered a through-hiker who once worked at the B&N Baked Bean factory in Boston. His job was to manually insert a piece of pork at the top of every

Thomas Knob shelter sits below the summit, fully exposed to Mt. Rogers' notoriously capricious weather. While here in April, two years earlier, I experienced a temperature drop from 40 to 20 degrees F, sudden 40 mph winds, and unexpected snow, over a period of 20 minutes!

filled can of beans passing by on the conveyor tracks, prior to its lid being applied and sealed. It was called "the Queen Bean".

View of a shrouded summit from Thomas Knob shelter. Three hundred yards behind the shelter is a fenced (against the feral horses) water source. Thirty yards "south" on the AT is an airy, composting latrine.

Raudy stands at the well marked junction of the AT and the Mt. Rogers Trail, which descends to Grindstone Campground, near our starting point on state highway 603.

The shady woodlands of the lower north slope of Mt. Rogers

Raudy takes a break at the marked junction of the Mt. Rogers Trail with the branch to Grindstone Campground. The alternative descent to the East, goes directly to state highway 602, about 2 miles west of the AT crossing and parking area.

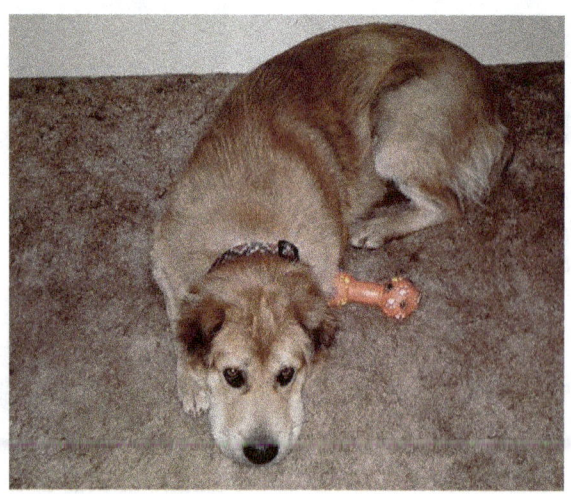

At home, an exhausted Shanghai adopts the "helpless baby fur seal" ploy.

April 2001: AT Duncan Ridge GA

Bob and Shanghai loop hike from AT
(5 days, ~55 miles)

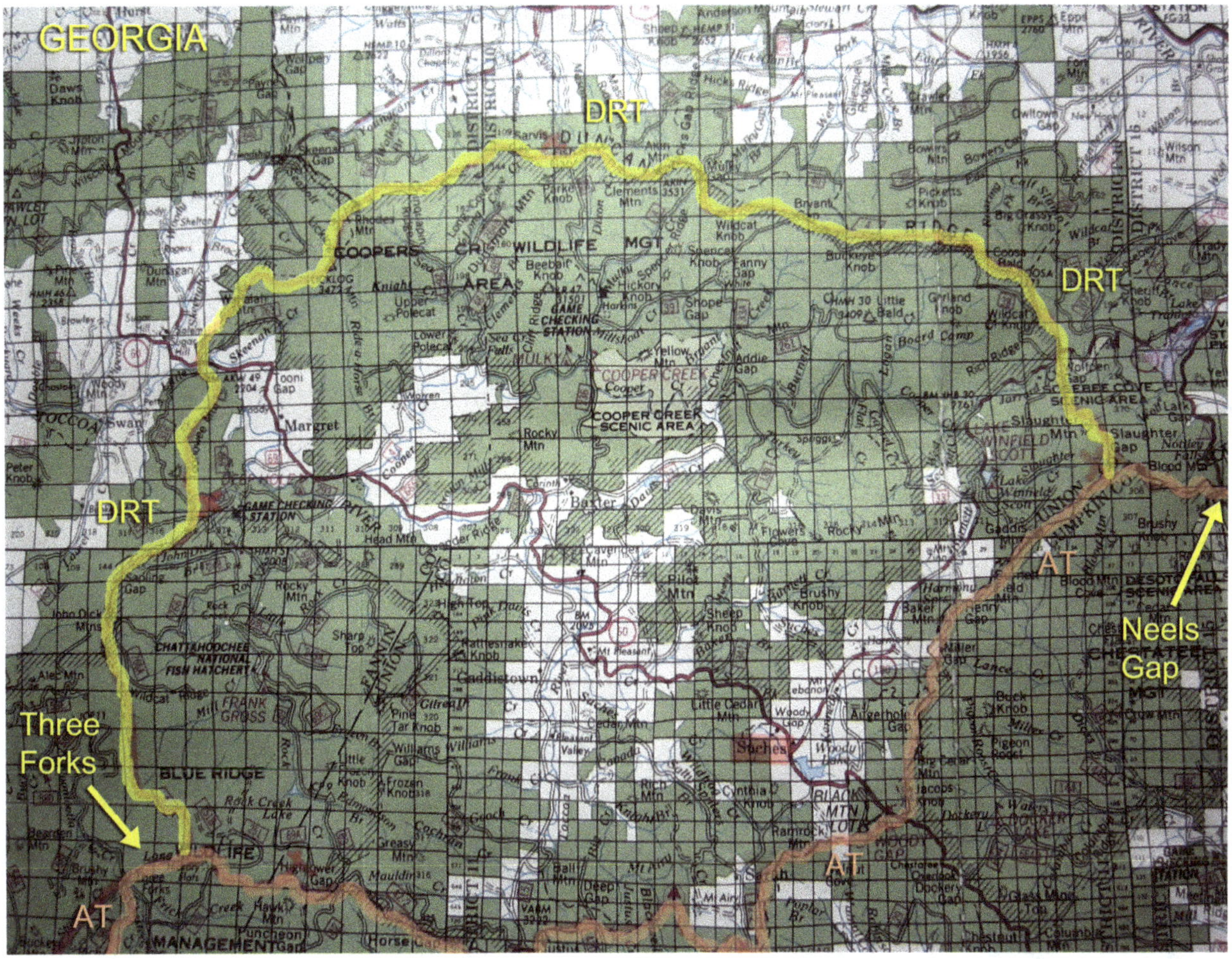

View from above Neels Gap.

My dog, Shanghai, and I departed a frigid, snow-covered southwest Virginia in mid-April, to drive in my old pickup truck to Georgia for this hike. It was about a six hour drive, including stops, to the parking area on the west of US 19, 1/2 mile north of Neels Gap, Georgia. The Appalachian Trail (AT) crosses US 19 at Neels Gap, actually passing through a building there.

Shanghai anticipated the hiking—since she celebrated my placing her red, doggie pack into the truck—by dancing in circles and leaping into the air. (That's quite a feat for a 100 pound dog with a stocky body and relatively short legs.)

Shanghai in her full rig. In order to provide a handle (for hauling her out of a creek) and a lead attachment at the rear of the pack, I stitched a nylon dog collar along its centerline. The lead is attached to a short bungee cord, to absorb any sudden tension.

Chattahoochee National Forest sign. An entire shelter for a sign, complete with benches.

The Duncan Ridge Trail (DRT) forms a loop off the AT in the mountains of Georgia. It turned out that the

At night, Shanghai was tethered with a 30-foot 1/8" braided nylon rope, positioned so that she could just barely make it fully inside my tent vestibule to lie down, if she chose. The tent is a Kelty Dart 1, single-wall, with a no-see-um mesh door between the vestibule and the interior. I find the tent quite uncomfortable to enter or exit, or even just to roll over inside, but it is light-weight.

A trail-side creek.

DRT was far more strenuous than I had anticipated.

DRT intersects with the AT at Three Forks. Hiking from the parking area 1/2 mile north of Neels Gap to Blood Mountain Shelter, we continued "south" on the AT to catch the bottom end of the DRT, then hiked the loop back to Blood Mountain.

Even though the trees of the north Georgia mountains had not yet leafed-out, the full sun brought hiking temperatures well into the mid 80s. With steep ups and downs (repeatedly gaining and loosing 400+ feet of elevation) and zero shade, I found the hike grueling, though beautiful and peaceful. Perhaps if my body had not still been in "winter mode", it might have been more comfortable. Shanghai still bore her dense, winter coat.

At most rest breaks, Shanghai's pack came off.

I had the DRT practically to myself, for my entire time on it. By contrast, the AT at this time of year is overpopulated and raucous, its shelters chaotic and full. So in that regard, the DRT was a better choice for hiking with a dog. Regardless, Shanghai was kept on a 10' lead attached to my pack harness with a climbers' short "quick-draw" strap (with a carabiner at either end). She seemed perfectly happy being always attached to me while hiking. At night, she was tethered to a tree with a 30' 1/8" braided nylon rope, positioned so that she could actually come into my tent's vestibule if she chose.

My Kelty Tioga pack and a pooped-out dog.

The length of the DRT itself has been estimated between 30.5 miles and 35.5 miles. I'll vote for the latter. Added to this was the half-to-one mile from the

Heating water for coffee.

parking area north of Neels Gap, up a side trail to join the AT at Blood Mountain Shelter, as well as the distance along the AT from the Blood Mountain Shelter to the DT's western (southern-ish) terminus with the AT (at a point where the DRT is sharing the treadway with the Benton McKaye Trail), at Three Forks. Altogether, I estimate a loop length of about 55 miles.

We take a break, before crossing the fantastical suspension bridge.

The most common view from the DRT.

For this hike, I decided in advance that I would cook no food. I would carry a stove and fuel only for making coffee in the morning. Instead of instant grits and oatmeal, and 7-minute noodle dinners, I carried along granola bars, PowerBars, candy bars, and various kinds of peanuts. After the third day out, as I was gagging on dinner, it finally occurred to me that everything—every bar of any ilk—was either peanut butter flavored, or contained peanuts. Peanuts. Peanuts.

Although the weather held for most of the trek, the final day on the DRT, ending at the campsite below Blood Mountain Shelter, was through torrential rain. Tethered to a tree with a 30' rope, Shanghai chose to go to its limit by coming into my Kelty Dart 1's vestibule to spend the night.

The trail gets consistently steep, both up and down. Shanghai would pull me uphill, but carefully provide slack in the lead on downhills.

Flat tentsites were easy to find.

Water is not easily located, and is usually a long way below Duncan Ridge.

The entire contents in each side of Shanghai's pack was surrounded by foam padding. She carried her food, 1 pt. of water, and a small, doggie towel, along with a fabric water bowl strapped on top.

The entirety of Duncan Ridge is a series of steep knobs. The trail summits every one.

On that last morning, we followed the AT "north", directly into Neels Gap, and the little souvenir store there. The AT passes beneath a portion of the building's roof. From there, we hiked the 1/2 mile north on US 19 to reclaim the pickup from the parking area. (Since my 1975 Ford pickup was the crappiest vehicle in the

I was there too.

Shanghai, rain-soaked, tangled and unhappy.

Blood Mountain Shelter in the rain. It was built by the Civilian Conservation Corp during the 1930's make-work program.

The AT passing through the building at Neels Gap. (Note the white blaze on the doorpost.)

parking area—by a wide margin, I had no concern that it might be stolen or vandalized. Its Virginia plates did easily mark it as belonging to a visitor.)

We drove north to the nearest Burger King. There I bought each of us a Whopper, and took them outside to eat. Only after Shanghai picked hers apart, then ate all but the big slice of onion, did I remember that onions don't play well with dogs. But Shanghai had that one figured out.

What turned out to be a hotter and more difficult hike than I had anticipated ended with my pickup truck breaking down as we made it back into southwest Virginia, but still nearly 60 miles from home. (The mountains had eaten my automatic transmission.) A kindly state trooper allowed Shanghai into the back seat of his cruiser, while he drove us to the nearest town.

There, I was able to arrange for a wrecker to transport the truck, with me in the wrecker's passenger seat, and Shanghai forlornly riding in the front seat of my disabled pickup, back to my home. She could see me inside the cab in front of her, and seemed to be comforted by that. The wrecker operator actually dropped me off right at my door, then off-loaded the dead pickup into my slightly snowy driveway.

Shanghai discarding the Wopper's onion.

There are many more trails to hike.

When I opened the door of the pickup, Shanghai leapt out with surprising energy, and again danced around in circles.

Winter 2003: AT Chestnut Knob VA

Bob and Richard on AT south of Burkes Garden VA
(2 days; 1.3 miles each way)

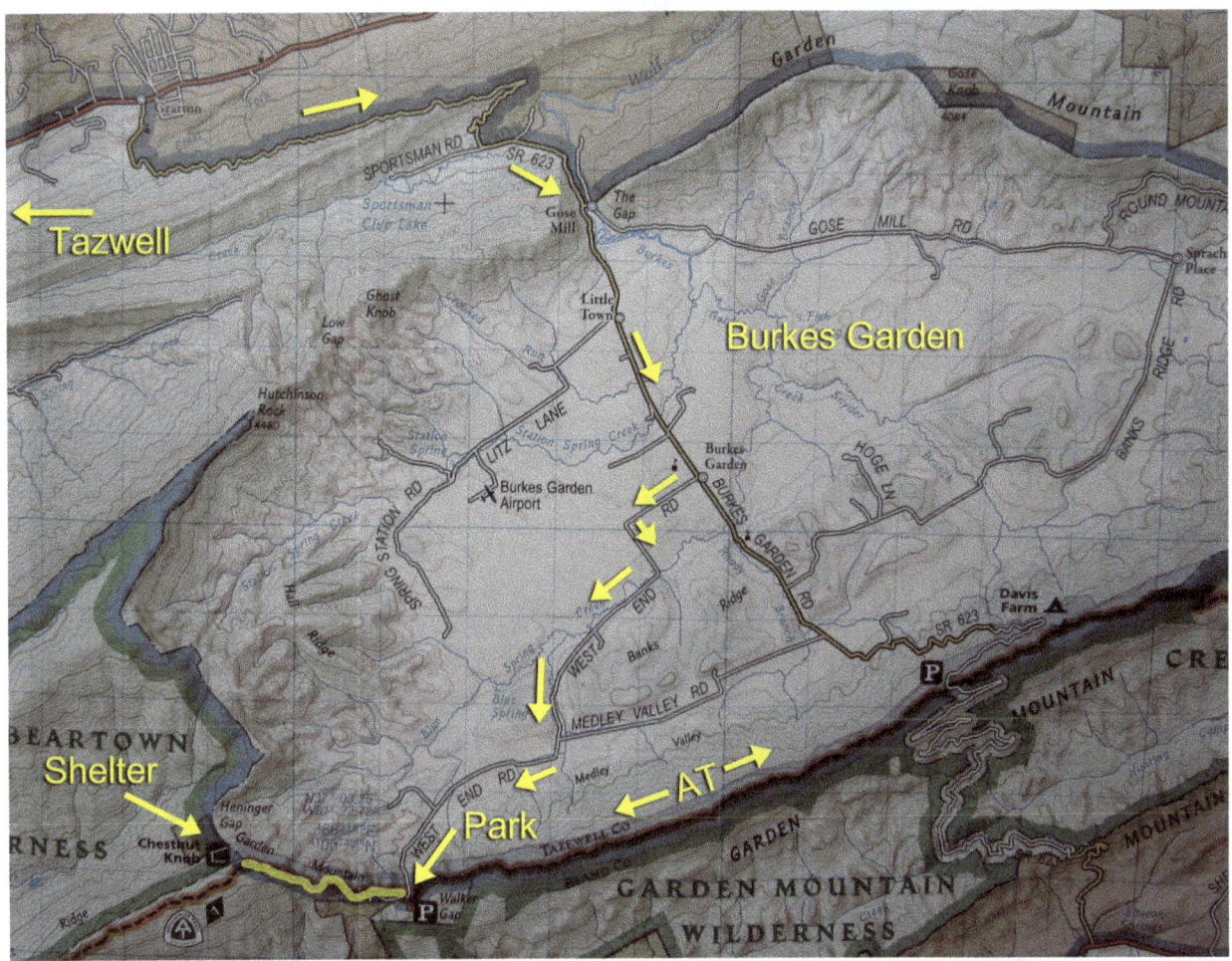

Burkes Garden is an impressively isolated community, in the geological sense. It is cradled within a deep, oval depression in the Appalachian mountain chain. I'm fairly confident that it is an impact crater, though the geologists I've consulted disagree, calling it a classic "sink". Regardless, the only practical way to reach Burkes Garden by automobile is by driving in from the north, along State Route 623. This winding highway comes off of VA 61, which comes off of US Business 19, east of Tazwell, VA. There is also a brutal, winding, gravel road (the southern end of Route 623) that goes from the south, up and over the high ridge enclosing the southern aspect of the depression, after crossing the Appalachian Trail (AT).

On Route 623, at the Post Office in Burkes Garden, county Route 727 comes off to the west. Following Rt. 727 for about 6 or 7 miles, making several turns along the way, we ended up going uphill on a steep gravel road (still Rt. 727) that dead-ends into the AT. There is a small parking area there and a spring nearby.

The dead end of Rt. 727. The AT crossing.

View of Burkes Garden from Chestnut Knob.

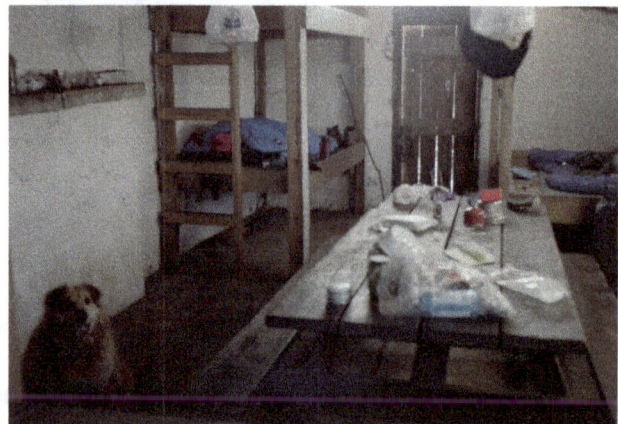

The interior of Chestnut Knob Shelter. Shanghai sits in front of the bricked-over fireplace. I'm standing on a bed platform with the camera. Note the "airy" door.

It is from this point that the AT, heading "south", goes up to Chestnut Knob on Garden Mountain, at the southwest extent of the oval ridge that surrounds Burkes Garden. The distance from the gravel road to Chestnut Knob Shelter is a mere 1.3 miles, but is a quite steep uphill nearly the entire distance.

Raudy asleep. Shanghai unhappy about the cold cement floor.

The shelter is a fully enclosed stone structure with a fireplace which, unfortunately, has been bricked over. It sits on a bald, exposed to the wind. In winter, at least while we were there, the wind was robust and cold. The building contains a table with benches, as well as two single, wooden bed frames and two double bunk frames. Room for six. Bring your own mattress and bedding! The wood bunks do keep a sleeper away from the frigid concrete floor.

Chestnut Knob Shelter.

Shanghai came along for this "short" overnight. We arrived at the AT crossing in mid-day, climbed up to the shelter, and cooked our dinners on our backpacking stoves at the handy table. Although I didn't record the temperature inside the shelter that night, I was somewhat cold inside my 15°F-rated sleeping bag (on the wood bunk, and on top of a Z-Rest pad).

Morning coffee, before returning.

Raudy writes in his journal, lift tickets at the ready. Noodle dinner packet is on the table.

There are panoramic views from the area of the shelter, but overall, it feels rather bleak in winter. In the morning, we made coffee and instant grits, then backtracked down the steep trail to our vehicle.

Micah at a campfire along the Iron Mountain Trail, summer of 2004.

July 2004: AT Iron Mountain TN

Bob, Richard, Micah, Floyd and Shanghai loop hike from Damascus VA along Iron Mountain Trail in TN to AT
(4 days; ~45 miles)

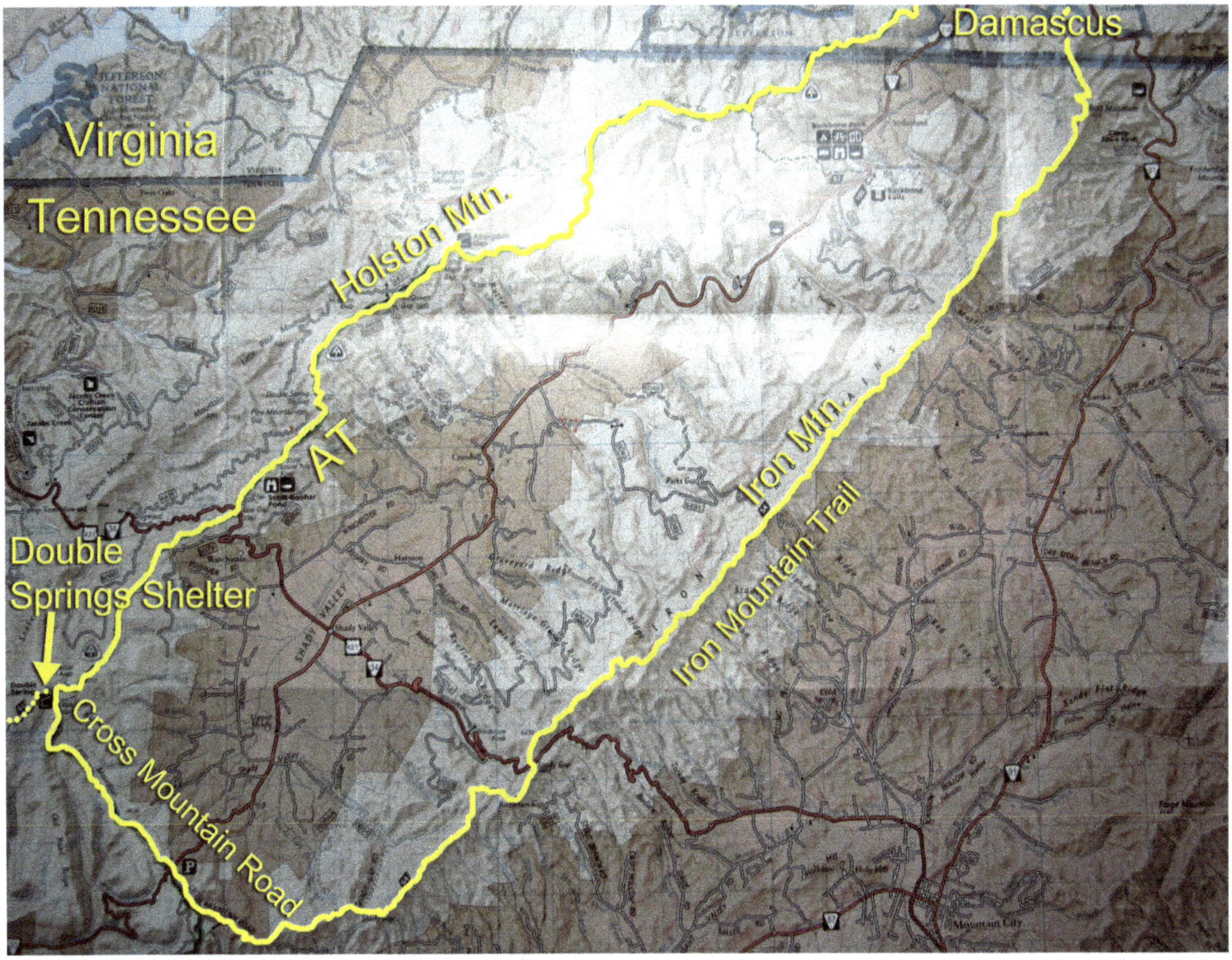

The ridge of Iron Mountain in Tennessee runs parallel to, and east of the path of the Appalachian Trail (AT) —along Holston Mountain—in northern Tennessee, and continues into southwest Virginia just east of Damascus, running from SW to NE. While the course of the AT currently switches to the east of Iron Mountain, and heads off toward Grayson Highlands and Mt. Rogers, that has only been since the AT was relocated several decades ago. Previously, the treadway passed along the ridge of Iron Mountain in Virginia. This obsolete, Virginia section of the AT is now named Iron Mountain Trail, and open for equestrian use, as well as for hikers. I have hike this

Micah and Shanghai on the IMT.

Holston Mountain and Iron Mountain are separated from one another by the long and relatively narrow Shady Valley. Shady Valley itself is closed off by a lovely section on a previous trek, but for the present trip, it is the *Tennessee* section of the Iron Mountain Trail (IMT) that we hiked.

An infrequent IMT trail blaze.

A natural fallen-tree sculpture.

Crossing US 421.

cross-ridge at its southwest extent. It is this cross-ridge, spanned by Cross Mountain Road, that connects the IMT to the AT, enabling a loop hike from Damascus VA.

Pack-off rest break.

On the single, bench seat of my old pickup truck, driving from the Blacksburg area to Damascus were myself (Stogie), my 26 year old son, Micah, and my eldest brother, Richard (Raudy). The long bed of the pickup contained our three backpacks, our walking sticks and poles, and the two dogs (safely tethered).

We parked our vehicle in a parking lot across from Mt. Rogers Outfitters, and, on this hot summer day, hiked with the two dogs (Shanghai and Floyd) along the town's streets to eventually reach the start of the southward bound IMT. We would later come to regret this decision to walk on the pavement for even this short a stretch.

Stogie, Shanghai and Micah. [RMG]

We stop for the first night.

About two miles south-east of Damascus, at the US 58 and VA 91 junction, the Iron Mountain trail begins, on its steep climb to the ridge line. The trail is not well marked, but is unmistakable. There are occasional blue blazes, or yellow diamonds at rare intervals. It climbs to the ridge, and stays there. This segment of

Micah sits on a ladder style.

Raudy and Floyd.

Raudy sets up camp.

Micah pitched his tent near Double Springs Shelter.

the trail is about 18 miles of nearly all uphill hiking. This was a difficult, though easy to follow path, camping before reaching Cross Mountain Road.

Most of the remaining three days of hiking would be either fairly level or the long, long downhill of the 18 mile descent of Holston Mountain on the AT into Damascus.

Stogie, Micah and Shanghai. [RMG]

The days were hot and sweaty, while the nights were comfortable. At each creek crossing, Shanghai and Floyd would always go into the creek and lie down, until forced to continue. (This later led me and Raudy to purchase little plastic wading pools at a big box store on the return drive, with the expectation that the dogs would enjoy lying in them on hot summer days. By the end of the summer, it was clear that neither

Floyd lost his right eye as a puppy, so only one reflects light.

dog was about to voluntarily step into a blue plastic pool of water. I suspect that, for Shanghai, it too closely resembled a mandatory "bath".)

Shanghai, feeling poorly.

Double Springs Shelter.

The line-up.

Official resting log.

Our second night, we camped in and around Double Springs Shelter on the AT. Unlike all my springtime hikes on the AT, by this point in the summer, there are very few AT through-hikers to be found in northern TN and southwestern VA, other than the occasional, south-bound hiker. So most of this four day hike was just us and the dogs.

Our final night was just north of Abingdon Gap Shelter, leaving about 10 miles—all downhill—to reach Damascus.

Surprisingly, as the hike progressed, the dogs seemed less and less eager to resume hiking after every rest break and every morning. It was not until I got home that I realized that Shanghai's rear paws were slightly swollen and tender. My guess is that the very first day, walking on the scorching pavement of Damascus, where the dogs dutifully followed us well-shod hikers, caused some heat injury to the pads of their paws. And those four days of hiking were probably not as enjoyable for them as one would have hoped. I felt terrible (and stupid) about it in retrospect.

View from Holston Mountain. [RMG]

Our final campsite on the Iron Mountain-AT loop.

Dog tired, beside her fabric water bowl.

Raudy makes dinner.

Morning smoke.

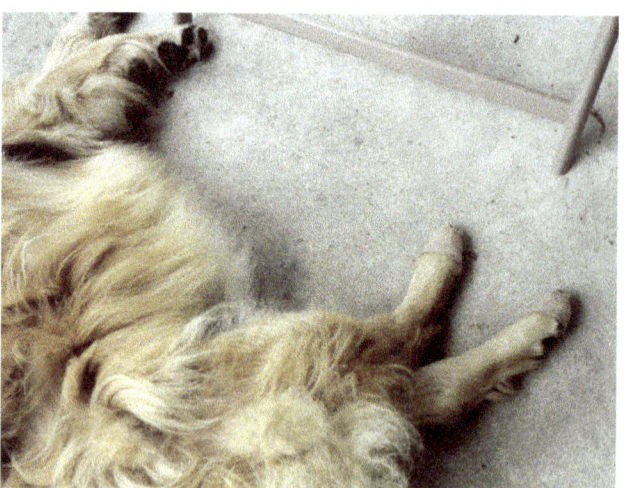
Shanghai with bandaged rear paws at home.

Shanghai seemed to be comforted by my belated application of Coban self-adhearing bandages to her paws. The dogs' affinity for lying down in every creek during this hike probably had been to diminish the pain, rather than to cool off.

2010 AT Dragon's Tooth VA July

Bob and Micah, day climb up and back

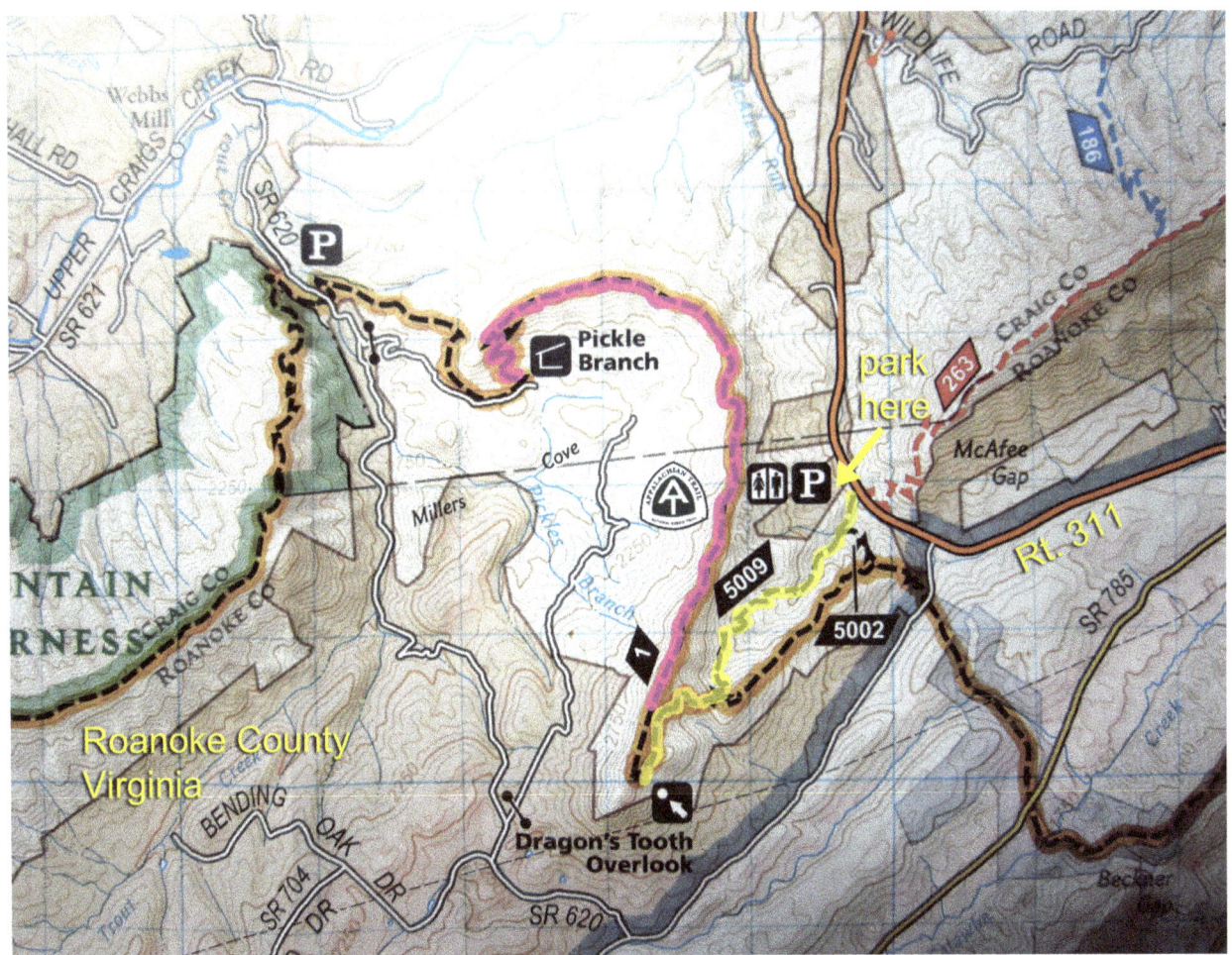

Dragon's Tooth Trail. Go north on Electric Road in Salem to reach Route 311. The yellow path is the day hike. The pink path continues on the AT to Pickle Branch Shelter, for an overnight.

Dragon's Tooth is a dramatic viewpoint along the Appalachian Trail (AT) in southwest Virginia, and is located north of Salem, VA. For a day hike, there is an access trail that leads from a parking lot just north of the Catawba Grocery, on VA 311 (the Electric Road exit on I-81). This access trail joins the AT (go "south") after less than 2 miles of flats and gentle slopes. The climb is a strenuous (~1200 feet of elevation, mostly toward the crest), roughly 4 to 5 mile hike in each direction, and requires some minor rock scrambling at one point near the top (with little sense of exposure). This cliff area makes the trail a challenge for a dog, though it is possible. Through-hikers with dogs regularly pass this part of the trail in both directions.

Stogie and Micah at the trailhead just south of the parking area off VA 311.

On reaching the flat crest of the mountain, Dragon's Tooth is to the left (west). Return by the same route (another 4 to 5 miles; 8 to 10 miles round-trip).

It is possible to climb the actual "Tooth", if you are courageous enough.

Micah looks north from the top of the trail.

The short hike can be made into a longer, overnight trek by following the AT "south" from Dragon's Tooth to Pickle Branch Shelter, 3.5 downhill miles farther. That makes a roughly 18 mile, 2 day round trip.

On weekends, when the weather is nice, there may be quite a few folks climbing to Dragon's Tooth. During weekdays, or during cold, dry, snow-free weather, solitude is more likely.

Raudy frames Lynn sitting atop the view at Angel's Rest, September 2012.

2012 AT Angel's Rest VA September

Bob, Richard and Lynn, day climb up and back

Angel's Rest is an Appalachian Trail (AT) viewpoint that floats above Pearisburg, VA, near the crest of Pearis Mountain, to the west of the town. At this point, the Appalachian chain is cleaved by the gap of the New River. So Pearis Mountain and its counterpart to the east, Peters Mountain are both at elevations considerably higher than the town. While the climb to Rice Shelter, on Peters Mountain is spread over about 6 miles, the far more abrupt climb on the AT "south" to Angel's Rest happens over a mere mile and a half, from where the AT crosses VA 793 (Cross Avenue). [Between the bridge at the New River, and VA 793 is a crowded congestion of businesses and backyards, and not much of scenic interest.]

A roadside pull-off at the point where VA 793 and the AT intersect is the place to park for a strenuous day trip up to Angel's Rest and back. This is a hike for cool weather or a summertime morning. We moved at less that 1/2 mph for the round-trip—6 hours!

Lynn ascends the stone steps in the easy section.

As a reward, the Dairy Queen rests at the bottom of VA 793 in Pearisburg.

Raudy.

I've hiked this a number of times in both directions, yet I never recall how tough the upper part of the climb turns out to be. There is a campsite about 1/2 mile further "south" on the AT, to make an overnight trip.

For this trip, my brother, Richard (aka Raudy) and my sister, Lynn (aka Lynn), joined me. This was Lynn's first exposure to a challenging segment of AT. By contrast, Raudy had sufficient experience to know and also to have forgotten how strenuous this hike is.

We drove up to Pearisburg from the Blacksburg area on a beautiful Sunday morning—the drive itself worth the time spent, parked at the pull-off on VA 634, and hiked our out-and-back. Lynn did really well for the climb up. She was tired, of course, but still in fairly good shape. Partway through the downhill return, her legs turned to rubber. Raudy and I carried her gear for the remainder of the descent. I suspect that she

Lynn and Raudy.

would have been fine if we had rested at the top for several hours, prior to descending. But there was some appointment for something later that afternoon.

The day (now mid-afternoon) was capped with a visit to the air-conditioned Dairy Queen, and the lovely ride back through the mountains that separate Pearisburg from Blacksburg, to return home.

Stogie. [RMG]

FLASHBACK: Raudy at Angel's Rest in July of 2010.

June 2013: AT Peters Mountain VA

Bob and Richard
(2 days; ~10 miles)

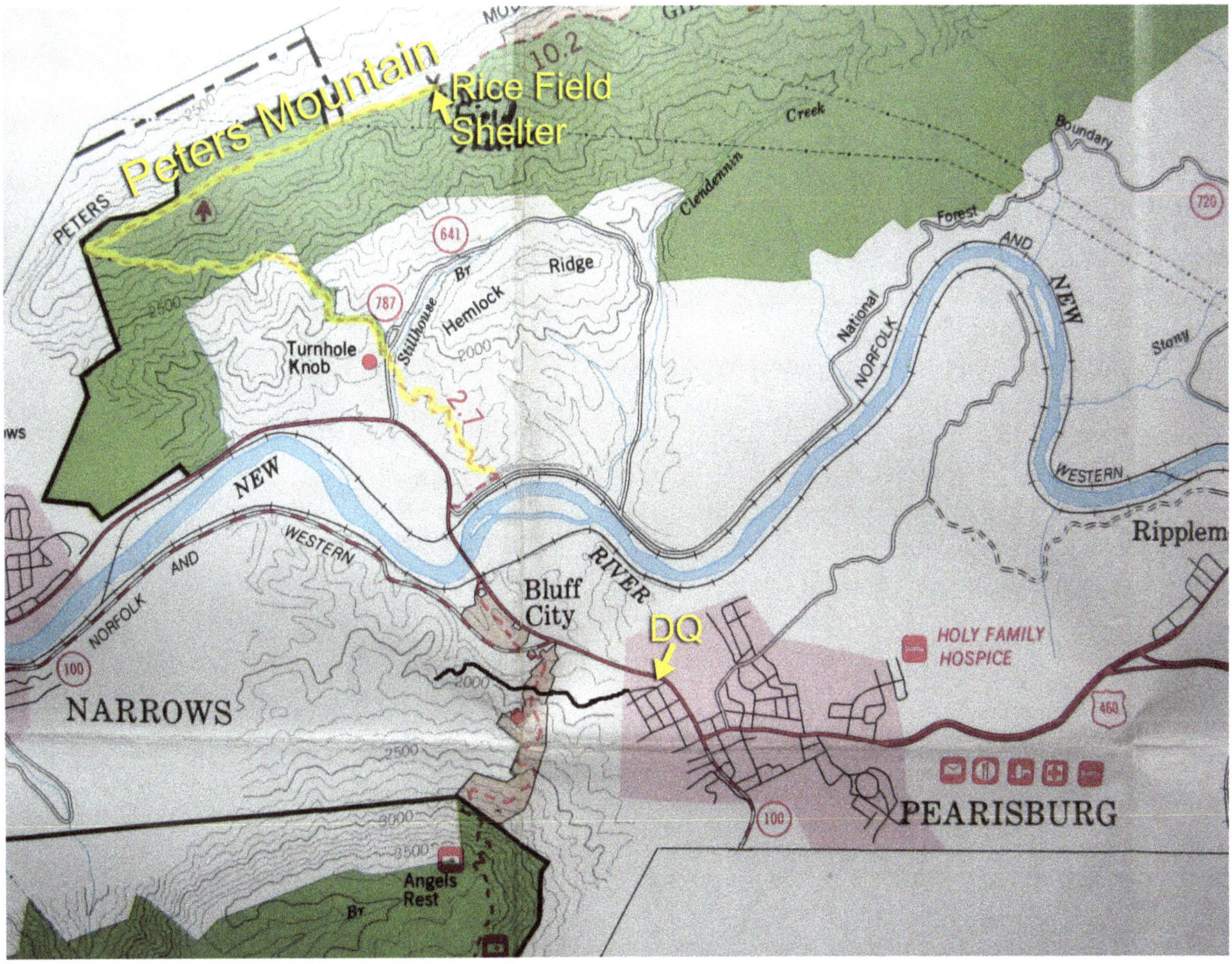

I (aka Stogie) and my brother, Richard (aka Raudy) decided to backpack up to Rice Field Shelter, along the crest of Peters Mountain, NE of Pearisburg VA. It is along the "north" direction of the AT, when leaving Pearisburg, and is a longer, though less strenuous hike than climbing to Angel's Rest, above the western side of the river.

We had encouraged our sister, Lynn, to come with us, but she had a laundry list of why she would be unable to take the time. So just the two of us.

Raudy's trekking poles. [RMG]

Stogie climbing the AT on Peters Mountain. [RMG]

We drove my old car up from the Blacksburg area on a sunny Saturday morning in early June. We crossed the New River bridge north of Pearsiburg, and turned east onto VA 641. The AT crosses this road, and that point offers a small off-road parking area to the north side. Being overly conscious of the weight that I was carrying, I looked at my car keys. They included an ignition key, a trunk key and a clunky, battery containing, electronic key fob more suitable for a woman's purse. Although I had never separated those keys, and always used the electronic gimmick to unlock the door, I hastily decided to leave the trunk key and the fat key fob, and just carry the remaining key. More on that later.

That trailhead lops about a mile off the distance to the shelter, but what it lops off is mostly flat. The trail meanders across a wide arc of the foot of Peters Mountain, before seriously tackling steeper terrain.

Pack-on break. [RMG]

Blue trillium with bright yellow anthers. [RMG]

We each brought our own tents, so we could leave the shelter for the footsore, AT thru-hikers that straggle in at all hours. Our packs were in the range of about 20 pounds each, including water.

Stogie sits in the vestibule of his single-wall, Kelty Dart 1 tent, pitched a short distance behind Rice Field Shelter. [RMG]

Raudy's Sierra Design Flashlight Tent. [RMG]

We (or I alone) must have appeared too frail to be engaged in this climb, because nearly every backpacker who passed us—and lots of them did—felt compelled to voluntarily point out to us how far the

View NE along the bald of Peters Mountain. [RMG]

View from Peters Mountain into West Virginia.

shelter is, and how terribly steep the trail becomes. Our uniform reply was, "Thank you. But we've hiked up there a number of times."

Words cannot explain. [RMG]

Rice Field Shelter is hidden in the trees. [RMG]

[I climbed up Peters Mountain in early April of 1997, to see Hale-Bopp comet, high in the sky over West Virginia. Once, I forget which year, Raudy and I climbed up there and lay on our backs in the bald, watching satellites pass overhead.]

View from the Scenic Privy. [RMG]

Raudy and Stogie. This ladder style is directly in front of the Shelter.

So we took our time—my time, actually, since I was considerably slower than Raudy. But we reached Rice Field Shelter (sometimes listed as Rice Fields Shelter or Star Gazer) with plenty of daylight remaining.

Stogie after the climb up. [RMG]

Rice Field Shelter. [RMG]

The views from the bald of Peters Mountain into West Virginia are unimpeded by vegetation, and there are no brightly-lit urban areas within the view—just a sprinkle of farms and homesteads. The bald itself has a scattering of sedimentary rock slabs hear and there, and is being encroached at the margins by thickets of American Hazelnuts. And there are broad brambles of blackberries, usually picked-clean by hikers.

The trail up from Pearisburg leaves no doubt that Peters Mountain was once an aquatic environment. All along the treadway one can easily spot all sorts of marine fossils, both tiny and fairly large.

Just Walking Home: Appalachian Trail Hikes 1996-2013

Stogie heading back toward Pearisburg. [RMG]

A fellow backpacker we were able to pass. [RMG]

Going downhill often required me to do a side shuffle. [RMG]

Although, as part of the AT, the trail is well blazed with the white rectangles on tree trunks—most in

This tree was likely bent over as a sapling, from a heavy tree falling onto it. [RMG]

sight of the next white blaze, it carries so much foot traffic that it is easy to follow. Our minds could focus on sharing a trek and making the climb.

An eastern fence lizard in the duff.

Stogie takes a pack-off break. [RMG]

After a quick breakfast and coffee, we headed back down. When we reached my car, ready for a trip to the Pearisburg Dairy Queen, I discovered to my everlasting embarrassment that the one car key that I had carried does not unlock the door. The "trunk" key does. And it was securely locked inside, beneath the driver's seat.

A large rock slab with fossils.

Raudy descends the trail.

Waiting along the highway for Lynn to rescue us with the spare keys.

I had an extra set of keys on top of my refrigerator, at home (10 miles south of Blacksburg). We phoned Lynn, and cajoled her to get the extra keys, and drive 40 miles to come and rescue us (and 40 miles back home). Raudy was furious at me. Lynn was furious at me. We walked out to the highway to wait. I thought senility was catching up with me. But as I write this six years later, it hasn't yet.

But the body has now, at the age of 71, rendered backpacking an activity that I can only write about with nostalgia. A lot of good times happened on the trail.

www.ingramcontent.com/pod-product-compliance
Lightning Source LLC
Chambersburg PA
CBHW080455170426
43196CB00016B/2822